£1.50
SMT

My Dear Son

Also by Colin Urquhart:

My Dear Son

A PERSONAL REVELATION OF JESUS

Colin Urquhart

Hodder & Stoughton
LONDON SYDNEY AUCKLAND

British Library Cataloguing in Publication Data

A catalogue record for this book is available from the British Library

ISBN 0-340-55809-1

Published by Hodder and Stoughton, a division of Hodder and Stoughton Ltd, Mill Road, Dunton Green, Sevenoaks, Kent TN13 2YA. Editorial Office: 47 Bedford Square, London WC1B 3DP. Photoset by Rowland Phototypesetting Ltd, Bury St Edmunds, Suffolk. Printed in Great Britain by Clays Ltd, St Ives plc.

For all who want
to know Jesus better.

Contents

Acknowledgments

My thanks are willingly given to all who have helped in the preparation of this book, especially to Anthea and Barbara for the countless hours spent on the word processor. And to Barbara and Helena for all their work in collating the scripture references.

I am so thankful to my wife, Caroline, for her loving patience whenever I have disappeared for a few days to write; for the times when I have been absorbed in the task or exhausted by it! Praise God for loving wives!

A Note for the Reader

It has been a great privilege and delight to receive so many testimonies, both verbally and by mail, telling how lives have been enriched spiritually through reading *My Dear Child*.

Many have related how their relationship with God has been strengthened; how they have received personal revelation of his love and acceptance. The Lord has used that book to speak directly into readers' personal circumstances.

My Dear Son is similar, yet different. For many years it has been my habit to spend time allowing the Lord to speak to my heart through the words of the Bible. I have found it immensely helpful to write down in the first person what he has said to me.

My Dear Son is a series of passages giving such personal revelation about the ministry of Jesus both during his incarnation and since.

I trust that you will find these pages helpful, that God will speak to you personally, revealing important truths to you about Jesus. I trust also that through using the book you will be prompted yourself to write down in the first person what you believe God is saying to you through passages of scripture.

My Dear Son is not intended to be a commentary, although your understanding of Jesus and his love for you will increase by reading this book. It is a series of inspirational meditations and should be used as such. May the Lord bless you and increase your faith in all he has done for you through Jesus.

Several scripture references are given for each section. These you can use for further study.

The phrase *My Dear Son* is ambiguous. It is used to speak of the way God wants to reveal the truth about Jesus to us. But it is also the way the Lord addresses all who have faith in him. We are all "sons of God through faith in Christ Jesus". That is true whether we are male or female, for we all share the first right of inheritance regardless of sex if Jesus is our Saviour and Lord.

When he speaks to me, he commonly uses the phrase "My dear son . . ." I have avoided using this in the text as I appreciate that many ladies would be more comfortable being addressed as daughter, even though they are also sons!

I have often used the word "Beloved". I suggest you insert the word "son" or "daughter" as appropriate – or your Christian name. At least know that these are pages addressed to you by the Lord who regards you as his "beloved".

1

Let There Be Light

— ○ —

"Through him all things were made; without him nothing was made that has been made. In him was life, and that life was the light of men."

(John 1:3–4)

Dear beloved child, the earth was formless and empty when I first spoke. Darkness covered the surface of the deep and my Spirit hovered over the waters.

"Let there be light." When I spoke, Jesus went forth from my mouth. He brought into being what was in my heart. Because I am light, I created light and I separated the light from the darkness. When I looked at what I had done I pronounced that it was good. Exactly what was in my mind had been brought into being. Jesus, my Word, had created what I wanted and I rejoiced in what he had done. He was with me before creation began; I have created nothing without him. He is God as much as I, your Father, am God.

In him was life and that life has become the light of men. I sent my light to shine into the spiritual darkness of the world. The Word through whom I had created became a man and lived within my creation. He came to bring the light so that men could know me. He came to reveal who I am and my purpose for my children.

You are my child because you have put your faith in Jesus. **I have spoken over your life and have said, "Let there be light." "Let light shine out of darkness."** His light has penetrated your spiritual darkness. Now I am your Father. I love you and I have separated you from the darkness of your past, so that you may walk in my light.

I want to show you why I sent Jesus. He reveals who I am and how much I love you. The more revelation you receive about him, the more of his light will shine into your heart. And you will grow in your understanding of all I have done for you through him.

John 1:1–5; Gen. 1:1–4; Eph. 5:8; Col. 1:12–13; 2 Cor. 4:6.

2

My Gift to You

———— o ————

"The Word became flesh and made his dwelling among us."

(John 1:14)

I selected carefully those I used for Jesus' coming:
Mary to be his mother; Joseph to be her partner;
Zechariah, Simeon and Anna to prophesy concerning
the child. He was born to be the Saviour of my people,
to rescue them from the hand of their enemies so they
could serve me without fear, in holiness and righteousness. He came to be a light for revelation to the Gentiles
as well as my people Israel.

He was born in humble circumstances. He didn't
come with pomp and majesty. His mission was to be a
servant coming to do for my people what they could
not do for themselves, drawing them back into fellowship with me. I longed for the time when I could live
not only among my people but within them.

Jesus came for those who knew their need of me; the
poor, the outcasts, the desolate, the broken-hearted,
the needy and destitute. He came with a message for
the wealthy, the worldly, the complacent. He came to
break through the bondage of religious legalism.

He came as a man, human, weak, open to temptation like any other man. Yet because of my divine

Spirit working perfectly within him, he lived a sinless life.

Dear child, as you trace with me the events of his life and ministry, understand how much you were involved in the things he did. **He lived for you. Whatever he said was to bring understanding to your heart. The events of his life are of dynamic significance for you. His words will bring you life, liberty and healing. You can put your complete trust in everything he has said. You can live in the victory of all he has accomplished.** This is my purpose for you.

He is my gift to you and to all my children. I don't want that gift wasted. Open your heart, understand and receive the great things I have done for you through Jesus. You see, I have also carefully selected you to be my child.

Phil. 2:6–7; Isa. 61:1–2; Heb. 4:16; John 6:68.

3

Jesus' Baptism

———— ○ ————

"This is my Son, whom I love; with him I am well pleased."

(Matt. 3:17)

He grew up in obscurity. It is not important for you to know the details of his formative years before his ministry began. John the Baptist prepared the path by calling my people to turn from their sins and return to my ways. By the time Jesus began his ministry there was already religious ferment in the land.

The people flocked to hear John. Many received forgiveness and the baptism he offered. Yet he was only the forerunner of the Messiah. He recognised his unworthiness compared with Jesus. So when Jesus came to the Jordan and asked to be baptised by him, John was reluctant at first. Yet when Jesus came out of the water, John saw the fulfilment of the prophetic vision he had received from me. He saw my Spirit descend on Jesus as a dove and heard my voice from heaven saying, **"This is my Son, whom I love; with him I am well pleased."**

Jesus is my Son. I am pleased with everything he said and did. If you truly want to please me, believe what he said and accept what he has done for you. I want you to live in the power of the life he came to give you.

So I say to you, dear child, as I said to Jesus: "You are my son, my child, whom I love. With you I am well pleased."

I am pleased, not because of your own accomplishments, for they have not brought you salvation or made you righteous in my sight. I am pleased with you because you have humbled yourself before me, have confessed your sins and received my forgiveness. **You have put your faith in Jesus and so I see you completely identified with him. You are clothed with his righteousness and destined to share his glory.**

You can rejoice that his love for you has made this possible.

Matt. 3:13–17; Matt. 3:1–3; Eph. 2:8.

4

It Is Written. . .

———— o ————

"Then Jesus was led by the Spirit into the desert to be tempted by the devil."

(Matt. 4:1)

After my Spirit had come on Jesus, he led him immediately into the wilderness to be tempted by the devil. Why?

Adam's sin had resulted in my people living in a spiritual wilderness. He had yielded to the devil's temptation by acting in disobedience to my word. Successive generations had inherited his sinful nature.

Jesus came as the new Adam. He was to undo the work of the first Adam. So in the wilderness he had to be subjected to Satan's temptations. Unlike the first Adam, **Jesus emerged triumphant. He resisted all temptation and obeyed my word.** He refuted the devil's attempts to seduce him into sin with the words: **"It is written . . ."**

All who do not follow Jesus still follow the first Adam. Because they have inherited his sinful nature, they yield to temptation and disbelieve the revelation of my truth All have sinned and fallen short of my glory.

Rejoice, child, that you live in the new Adam and not the old one. You now have a new nature: Christ in

you, the hope of glory. In him you are able to resist temptation and to believe my word.

Beloved, you are to live on **every** word that comes from my mouth.

It is not for you to disregard what I say, choosing to believe only what you want. I don't submit my word to you that you might judge what I say with your limited understanding. No, beloved, you are to submit your mind to my word so that I can inform you of the truth.

My truth will set you free and show you how to live using all the supernatural resources I make available to you.

When tempted to disbelieve what I say, you can answer like Jesus: "Away from me, Satan!"

Matt. 4:1–11; Rom. 5:12–17; Rom. 3:23; Col. 1:27; John 8:32.

5

Your Wilderness

———— o ————

"We do not have a high priest who is unable to sympathise with our weaknesses, but we have one who has been tempted in every way, yet was without sin."

(Heb. 4:15)

J esus had to experience every temptation possible. **He identified completely with you, so you can identify completely with him.** Just as my Spirit led Jesus deliberately into the wilderness, so I lead you into the wilderness, not because I am angry with you but to strengthen your faith. Such times bring refining into your life and teach you to trust me regardless of your circumstances. And that is one of the most important lessons for you to learn, beloved.

The wilderness is a desolate place. It seems there is nothing to sustain or encourage you. You feel isolated and alone. There is nobody to turn to, no one who can understand your predicament – except me! This is why I allow such times. Each of my children has his or her times in the wilderness. Either they emerge with a stronger trust in me, or they fall away because they follow me for the wrong reasons. The enemy is very active in his attempts to lure them away from dependence on me.

During these times you see your own heart more clearly. You have to ask yourself: do you really trust me, or do you try to struggle through in your own strength?

As with Jesus, I have supplied all the resources you need to withstand everything and anything the enemy throws against you. Like Jesus, you can come through every time of testing victoriously. Like Jesus, I want you to emerge from your time in the wilderness full of joy in the Holy Spirit.

Do you understand? I have given you my Spirit to lead you through every time of difficulty in triumphant joy. Even during wilderness experiences, I promise both my presence and provision. I hear your cry for help and answer you. It is never my purpose to leave you in the wilderness.

So don't resent these times. They are times of refining and opportunities for spiritual growth, even when it seems I am far from you. When you have trusted me in the wilderness, you can trust me anywhere.

Heb. 4:14–16; Ps. 66:10; Rom. 8:6; Ps. 139:7–10; Jas. 1:2–4.

6

The Word of Life

———— o ————

"For the word of God is living and active."

(Heb. 4:12)

Dear child, imagine the power of my Word that formed the creation all around you. That same Word that brought the entire universe into being became a man. No wonder Jesus spoke with authority! No wonder he said his words were Spirit and life. No wonder he could heal every form of sickness and deliver people from demonic powers, simply through speaking words of command.

Jesus didn't begin his existence as a baby in Bethlehem; he was with me in the beginning. He has been the Word that has gone forth from my mouth since time began.

I want you to understand, therefore, that Jesus is my Word throughout the Bible. I speak through the Old Testament prophets and the history of my people Israel. I speak through the humanity of Jesus. I speak through the Holy Spirit in the writings of the apostles! The whole Bible, therefore, has my authority and is the revelation of truth.

"All scripture is God-breathed . . . so that the man of God may be thoroughly equipped for every good work."

Spiritual truth cannot be known through reason or opinion, only by revelation. I revealed the truth about myself and what I required of my people through the law and the prophets.

I revealed the truth about myself and the nature of my Kingdom through my Son.

I revealed the way my Holy Spirit works in the lives of my children through the apostles.

Beloved, I want you to be glad you have this revelation of truth. Treat my word with the respect it deserves. Honour the authority with which I have spoken as your Lord and God. Believe my words and my truth will set you free. This is my promise to you. I don't want you to live in a wilderness of your own making because of your unbelief.

John 1:1–3,14; 1 Thess. 2:13; 1 Pet. 1:23–5; John 8:31–2; 2 Tim. 3:16–17.

7

Rejected For Me

———— o ————

"The Spirit of the Sovereign Lord is on me, because the Lord has anointed me . . ."

(Isa. 61:1)

The wilderness was only the beginning of the testings and trials Jesus experienced. He was rejected by members of his own family, his village and by members of the synagogue where he worshipped.

In the synagogue at Nazareth Jesus read from the scroll of Isaiah. My Spirit had anointed him to fulfil this prophecy. He was the One I had sent to preach good news to the poor, proclaim freedom for prisoners and recovery of sight to the blind; to release the oppressed and proclaim the year of my favour. And my Spirit would enable him to fulfil this purpose.

In the wilderness, Satan tried to encourage him to misuse his anointing for his own ends. Having resisted that temptation, Jesus set about the task for which he was sent.

People were amazed at the way he spoke under the anointing of the Holy Spirit. How could a carpenter's son possibly be the One I had sent as their Messiah? Even his own brothers didn't believe in him.

You have found it frustrating and disappointing when those close to you have rejected what you believe. They don't want to hear the truth. In rejecting me it seems they reject you, doesn't it? I understand, my child. This is part of the cost of communicating the truth to those full of unbelief.

It hurts, doesn't it? You feel sad for those who reject me because you know that unless they turn to me, they will miss the life only I can give. The truth alone can set them free.

Jesus was never deterred by rejection; he knew I would never deny my Son. I would never fail him. He was secure in my love. The works he performed, as well as the words he spoke, pointed to his true identity. He made it clear that he could do nothing himself. He did what he saw me doing and spoke the words I gave him to speak.

I don't want you to be deterred by rejection either. **I will be with you always. I will never deny you or fail you. I will supply all you need to be my faithful witness. Your security is in my love for you; I have accepted you.** Your status has nothing to do with whether people accept or reject you. You are in Jesus, and he in you, regardless of the way others treat you!

Luke 9:22; John 15:18–21; 1 Pet. 2:4; 1 Pet. 4:12–16; 2 Pet. 1:3.

8

New Wine

———— o ————

"You have saved the best till now."

(John 2:10)

W hy should Jesus change water into wine? Was this simply an act of love that enabled a wedding party to continue? No, this event had much greater significance. Everything Jesus did had meaning beyond the event itself.

The law was like the wine that ran out. It was good in itself but was about to be superseded by something far better. The law revealed to my people what I demanded of them; but it possessed no power to enable them to do my will. It pointed the way to righteousness but could not make anyone righteous.

With the coming of Jesus it was time for new wine. He came not to give law but life. He came to make my people righteous and to give them the power they needed to do my will.

Those who tasted this new wine immediately noticed the difference in quality from the old. Jesus offered this new wine of eternal life first to those who were familiar with the old. He came to those who had lived under the law, but made it clear that eternal life was my free gift to any who put their faith in him. Whoever believes in Jesus, Jew or Gentile, will enjoy the heavenly marriage supper I have prepared. How sad that many refused the salvation and life he alone could give!

Many who call themselves Christians today taste something of the truth through their religious traditions; but when they are offered new wine, the life they can receive through entering into a real relationship with me, they begin to excuse themselves. However, those who come to a living faith wonder why the new wine was kept until now. Why have they been offered only religious practices and services when Jesus came to give them life?

It is difficult for old wineskins to contain this new wine. Old traditional structures become stiff and unyielding to the presence of my Spirit, limiting what I do among my people. Even when my Spirit moves in power and breaks the boundaries men have set, they soon want to reassert their control and impose restrictions on me, telling me what I am allowed to do and when!

Beloved child, drink deeply of this new wine of my love; all the resources of my new life are yours. Just as I made wine out of ordinary water, so I turn ordinary lives like yours into new wine. I have made you a new creation.

Know that when people taste the new wine of my presence in your life, they are greatly blessed.

John 2:1–11; John 10:10; Acts 1:8; Eph. 1:3.

9

Born Again

———— ○ ————

"I tell you the truth, no-one can see the kingdom of God unless he is born again."

(John 3:3)

The miracles Jesus performed created much interest, even among the religious leaders. One of them called Nicodemus came to him secretly at night, recognising that Jesus could only do such things because God was with him.

Jesus told him that no one can see my Kingdom without being born again. To be born physically is not sufficient. People can try to serve me with their natural lives, but this does not give them eternal life or enable them to inherit my everlasting Kingdom. They must have a second birth, a spiritual birth.

This was a new way of thinking for Nicodemus. He failed to realise that this was my way of fulfilling my promise to give my people new hearts and put my Spirit within them.

The Jews were expecting their Messiah to come, but not as a Servant! They wanted a political liberator, not a sacrifice for sin.

They wanted my Kingdom to come but didn't understand that my reign would be established in hearts and lives through the new birth. Jesus explained that this was the only way by which men could be saved from the condemnation they deserve because of their sin and rebellion, their failure to meet the righteous demands of the Law. He came to save the world; anyone of any generation, nation, background and culture who put their faith in him.

Without faith in what he did on the cross, a person is already condemned. Jesus came as light into the world; but those who reject the light remain in darkness.

Many of the leaders believed their religious zeal was the light; yet when Jesus showed them the true light they rejected him. They didn't realise that the law they observed was only a shadow of the things to come. They feared breaking with tradition and being judged by their contemporaries.

Those who recognise Jesus as the truth put their trust in him, and so receive life in all its fullness. Beloved, **you received this new birth when you heard the good news of salvation through Jesus and believed in him. Then I gave you the Holy Spirit to live within you; and he is the guarantee of your inheritance.**

You recognise Jesus as the truth and he has filled you with his light. You don't need to fear breaking with tradition or being judged by your contemporaries. It is better to belong to the truth than to be filled with lifeless religious zeal. Dear child, I rejoice that I live in you by the presence of my Holy Spirit!

Ezek. 11:19–20; John 5:24; John 5:39–40; 1 John 2:20–1.

10

The Life of The Kingdom

———— o ————

**"For the kingdom of God is . . . righteousness, peace
and joy in the Holy Spirit."**

(Rom. 14:17)

I gave Jesus the commission to take the good news
of my Kingdom throughout Israel. I wanted my
people to receive my Kingdom as a gift by believing Jesus
to be my Son. They had to repent of their sins and
acknowledge him as their Lord. They couldn't receive
the life of my Kingdom without turning from their
rebellion and disobedience. They couldn't put the
new life on top of the old. They must be freed from
the old, then they would be free to live the new
life.

Dear child, to be sorry for sin is not enough. When
people repent they have to turn away from their life of
sin. Only then can they receive the life of my Kingdom;
only then can I establish my reign in them.

Jesus revealed the nature of that Kingdom. It is a reign
of love, received only through my grace and mercy.
It is a Kingdom of supernatural power, a Kingdom of
righteousness and justice.

Those who are part of this Kingdom are to express its
life – like Jesus did. **I want to see love reigning in their
lives. I want them to use the power and authority of**

this Kingdom; to live in righteousness and to be concerned for my justice to be brought to the nations.

You can understand why people were perplexed. To them Jesus was merely a man. What man could offer such a Kingdom, unless he was the Son of God? They had little evidence at this stage as to his true identity. That would not be the case for long, for the works he performed verified the message he proclaimed.

Those who heard Jesus and believed were called to be his disciples. From the beginning some had to face the cost of leaving their jobs and families to travel with him from place to place. He used no persuasion. He simply said, "Follow me," and they left everything. They didn't know what lay ahead of them, but with child-like trust they followed.

I have chosen to give you my Kingdom, beloved child. You have turned from your life of sin and put your faith in Jesus, haven't you? Now I want the life of my Kingdom to be expressed increasingly in you.

Let love reign in your heart at all times; then love will be expressed in whatever you say or do. I want you to be merciful to others as I have been merciful to you. Remember that you have all the power and resources of my Kingdom available to you as you exercise the faith and authority I have given you. You can walk in righteousness and justice. You are to reign in life as a child of the King. I want to teach you how to do this.

John 3:16; Matt. 4:19–20; Mark 1:22; Mark 16:17; Rom. 5:17.

11

I Exalt The Humble

———— o ————

"He . . . has lifted up the humble. He has filled the hungry with good things."

(Luke 1:52–3)

My Spirit came upon Mary and she conceived. During her pregnancy she prophesied that my mercy extends to all of every generation who fear me. I bring down rulers, removing them from their thrones, but I lift up the humble. I fill those who are hungry with good things, but the rich I send away empty.

Do you understand these things, child? If you are hungry for the truth, I will feed you. If you want to be righteous in my sight, I alone enable that. If you want my will for your life, I fill you with the riches of my Spirit.

By contrast, those who trust in themselves, in their wealth, their own opinions and intellectual prowess, I send away empty. It is not that I am opposed to the intellect or to wealth. I created the intellect; the earth and everything in it is mine. But when people put their confidence in their intellectual ability or material prosperity, they oppose the revelation of my truth and don't put their trust in me.

Jesus humbled himself to bring salvation; only those who humble themselves before me receive that salvation. Those who turn to me in repentance and put their faith in Jesus shall reign in this life and enjoy my glory eternally.

Beloved, understand that this is my purpose for you. Feed daily on my words. I want to give you understanding of what I have done for you through Jesus.

Don't listen to any who would try to undermine the revelation of my word because of their unbelief. Don't listen to those who explain away the supernatural elements of the gospel. I will never be limited by the natural.

My supernatural life invaded the natural world when Jesus became a man. He lived the life of my supernatural, eternal Kingdom on earth. It is impossible to live my kingdom life by your natural understanding and power. **When you were born again, the supernatural life of my Holy Spirit invaded your natural life so that you too could live the life of my Kingdom.**

Because you have humbled yourself before me, child, I have lifted you up. You were hungry and I have fed you with good things. Yes, I have chosen the foolish of the world to shame the wise, the weak to shame the strong. No one can boast before me!

Luke 1:46–55; Matt. 1:22–3; 1 Cor. 1:27; Col. 3:16; Jas. 4:10.

12

My Kingdom In You

———— o ————

**"The kingdom of heaven is like a mustard seed . . .
Though it is the smallest of all your seeds, yet when it
grows . . . [it] becomes a tree."**

(Matt. 13:31–2)

J esus likened my Kingdom to treasure in a field, or a
pearl of great price. Nothing could be more valuable
than possessing my Kingdom, for when you do so all
the resources of heaven are yours to be used to good
effect in your life.

The Kingdom is not a piece of land but my reign
within those who believe in me. Because the Kingdom
is within you, all the riches of that Kingdom are within
you. I chose to give you the Kingdom, not as a reward
for self-righteousness, but as my gift to you; a work of
my grace.

Jesus likened my Kingdom to a seed planted in the
ground. When someone gives their life to me, that seed
is planted in their heart and it begins to grow, first the
blade, then the ear, then the full corn in the ear.

The life of my Kingdom has been planted in you,
dear child. Even now it is growing. As this process continues, more of my life will be manifested in the kind
of person you are and the things you do and say.

The sower sowed the seed of my word. When it fell on the path, people rejected the revelation Jesus came to give. When it fell on rocky soil, people at first received the word because they thought it would bring them blessing. But they didn't live for the truth; my word was not rooted in them. When under pressure they believed their own feelings and reactions to their problems instead of believing my promises. What was planted in them withered instead of growing to fruitfulness.

In others the seed of my word becomes choked by weeds: worry, anxiety and cares about money. The deceitfulness of wealth chokes the life of the Kingdom within a person. He imagines his prosperity depends on what he possesses rather than on what I give him. Or he thinks he can live the life of the Kingdom, while trying to withhold certain things from me.

In the good soil, the seed grows to full maturity and produces thirty, sixty and a hundred times what was sown. **Dear child, if you hold fast to my word with a good and honest heart, you will bear much fruit. You will prosper and flourish as a child of my Kingdom. You will spread Kingdom seeds all around you.**

Be thankful that you have received the Kingdom. Let the seed grow to full maturity unhindered. Root out immediately anything in your life that is a contradiction to my reign in you. I cannot reign in pride or selfishness, in anger, bitterness or malice, in jealousy or laziness, or any form of unrighteousness.

Beloved child, people will increasingly see the evidence of my life and power in you as you seek first my Kingdom and my righteousness.

Matt. 13:44–6; Matt. 13:11–12; Luke 17:20–1; Matt. 13:1–9; Eph. 4:29; Col. 3:5–14.

13

The Riches of My Kingdom

———— ○ ————

"'My son,' the father said, 'you are always with me, and everything I have is yours.'"

(Luke 15:31)

Beloved, I am merciful; so mercy is one of the principles of my reign.

In the parable of the two brothers, the lost son wasted his inheritance. The father gave him what he asked, because he was entitled to his inheritance even though he chose to waste it. From a luxurious lifestyle, he descended to eating the food of the pigs he fed. He realised it would be better to return to his father, though he considered himself no longer worthy to be called a son. He was prepared to be treated as a hired servant. That would be better than eating pigs' swill.

When his father saw him coming, he ran to meet him and embraced him with forgiveness, love and acceptance. He ordered that he be given a fine robe, shoes for his feet, and a ring for his finger. The fatted calf was to be killed for a celebration feast.

His elder brother also wasted his inheritance, but in an entirely different way. He never claimed it! He resented the celebration that greeted his brother's return and refused to join the dancing and feasting. He complained that his father had never given him even a baby goat to have a feast with his friends.

Do you remember what the father said to him? "Son, you are always with me. Everything I have is yours."

Because you are my child you have a rich inheritance. Don't misuse it by walking in the flesh instead of in the power of my Spirit. Neither be like the elder boy who didn't lay claim to his inheritance. **Everything I have is yours. The more you lay claim to the resources of my Kingdom, the more I rejoice.** Use those resources to the full and you will be fruitful in encouraging others to embrace me and my Kingdom.

And you will never be resentful of those who dance in celebration of my goodness! You will enjoy the feast yourself!

Luke 15:11–32; Lam. 3:22–3; Eph. 1:18.

14

Dispel the Darkness

———— o ————

"Zacchaeus, come down immediately. I must stay at your house today."

(Luke 19:5)

When he repented Zacchaeus wanted to restore all he had taken by deception and fraud. Salvation came to his house because Jesus came to his house!

Beloved, Jesus was prepared to mix with sinners, reaching out to them with love and forgiveness. They needed to hear the good news of the Kingdom, to be given the opportunity to repent and put their faith in him.

The religious leaders couldn't understand why Jesus ate with social outcasts or a swindler like Zacchaeus. He was prepared to go in holiness wherever there was impurity. He wanted to cleanse the impure and offer them life. He took his light into the darkness, his peace into turmoil, his compassion where there was mourning and grief. He took healing where there was sickness, deliverance where there was bondage. He didn't avoid sinners; he embraced them in his love.

Jesus made it clear that some prostitutes and swindlers were entering the Kingdom before the religious ones who preferred their traditions to the life he

offered. They were content with their self-righteousness instead of receiving true righteousness which comes through repentance and faith in Jesus.

Every sinner needs to hear the truth and the offer of salvation I make. I lead my disciples where religious people would never go. I send them wherever there is need. My Holy Spirit leads them to take my life where it is both needed and will be welcomed.

Beloved child, today I come where there is great need. I come to the lost, to those who have known depravity, to those who feel totally unacceptable, outcasts of society. I come to those who feel weak, who consider themselves failures.

I come to those who have been lulled into false security by their religious traditions and practices. Regardless of their former lives, I make all who turn to Jesus one in him; they share the same life and have the same inheritance.

As my child, you share the life of my Kingdom with all who are my sons and daughters, irrespective of their former lives. What they were doesn't matter to me and is not to matter to you. It is what I have made you all that is important.

So, beloved, live in the good of who you are now. Never mind what you used to be!

Luke 19:1–10; Matt. 21:31; Matt. 9:12–13; 2 Cor. 5:17.

15

Your Eternal Destiny

————— o —————

"Today, if you hear his voice, do not harden your hearts."

(Heb. 3:15)

There was a rich man and a poor beggar at his gate named Lazarus. The wealthy one had everything he needed in this life; the beggar had nothing. When Lazarus died, angels carried him to a place of peace in Abraham's bosom. But when the rich man died he was cast into the fire of judgment. There was a great chasm between them that could never be crossed.

People forge their eternal destiny by the way they live in this life. Many believe they can leave reconciliation with me to the last minute, or that they will receive a second chance beyond death. Beloved, do everything you can to show the fallacy of this thinking. There will be no second chance. Why should I come into the world if it was possible for people to be saved after they had left this world?

Today is the day of salvation. Now is the opportunity for people to secure their eternal destiny by putting their faith in Jesus. I have sworn that those who harden their hearts against me shall never enter my rest.

The rich man wanted Lazarus to return to earth to warn his relatives of their impending peril. If people don't believe my own Son, they will certainly not listen to anyone else!

Beloved child, keep praising me for my anger has turned away from you. **Jesus has suffered the punishment you deserved. I am your salvation. You do not need to fear judgment.** I am your strength and your song. With joy you will draw water from the wells of salvation.

So shout aloud and sing for joy because of the glorious things I have done for you!

Luke 16:19–31; Heb. 9:27–8; Isa. 12:1–6.

16

Follow or Reject

———— o ————

**"With man this is impossible, but with God all things
are possible."**

(Matt. 19:26)

My beloved, the way of salvation is a Person. Truth
is a Person. Life is a Person: JESUS! He is the only
way that anyone can come to me as their Father. **The
truth is found only in him. He is the only source of
eternal life.**

Jesus was the way for Peter, John, James and all the
other disciples; for Nicodemus, and the woman caught
in adultery; for Mary Magdalene who was delivered
from demonic powers, and for many others.

Many Pharisees, Sadducees and lawyers rejected him
as the way. They were more interested in retaining their
religious authority and holding on to their own perspective of truth. So they rejected and crucified the way, so
great was their self-righteousness.

Others rejected the truth because it seemed too costly.
The rich young man was more in love with his riches than
with me. Many made excuses when Jesus called them to
take up their cross, deny themselves and follow him.

Dear child, today many embrace my life and experience my forgiveness and acceptance. They are glori-

ously transformed and liberated; I even work miracles in their lives. Others reject me and so reject the life and heavenly inheritance that otherwise could be theirs.

Jesus made it clear that he came to bring division. His words were like a double-edged sword that cut to the heart. Even within families there would be division between believers and those who rejected him as the truth. Such things are inevitable as each person has to be free to make a personal response to him.

It angers me to see religious leaders not only refusing to receive the life I offer, but also hindering others from receiving. They are accountable to me for their actions. They teach others to beware of being born again and being filled with my Spirit. They dismiss the genuine moving of my love in the hearts of people as mere emotionalism. They give the impression that all will be saved in the end, without any regard for what Jesus teaches.

They say that I would not reject anyone because I am love. **Certainly I would like all to be saved. That would only be possible if all believed.** Those who persist in hardening their hearts against me have made their choice. They will remain in condemnation and under the judgment of my wrath unless they repent and believe the good news.

I cause heaven to rejoice whenever a sinner realises his need and turns to me. Even those religious leaders who have led others astray will receive mercy, not judgment, when they turn to me themselves. Instead of their pride, self-righteousness and fear of man, they will receive my abundant life.

Dear beloved child, it is unloving to compromise the truth of my gospel. Don't agree with the opinions of men to gain popularity with them. Hold fast to the truth; then you will be popular with me!

John 14:6; John 3:10; Heb. 4:12; Matt. 10:34.

17

You Are Blessed

———— o ————

"Blessed are those who hunger and thirst for righteousness, for they will be filled."

(Matt. 5:6)

Beloved child, you are blessed. You are happy because you have found your fulfilment in me.

You are blessed because you have recognised your need of me. The Kingdom of heaven is yours.

You are blessed because you have grieved over your past sin and failure to please me. I have comforted you with my forgiveness and with the presence of my Holy Spirit coming to live within you.

You are blessed as you walk humbly before me and others. You are able to share in Jesus' inheritance, for he is gentle and humble in heart.

You are blessed because you have hungered and thirsted after righteousness. You have been filled with the living water of my Holy Spirit.

You are blessed because, having experienced my mercy, you are merciful towards others. Therefore I continue to show you my mercy.

You are blessed because I have given you a new heart. I have taken out the heart of stone and given you a heart that pulsates with my love. As you live in the purity of that new heart you shall see me, your holy God.

You are blessed whenever you reach out to people to draw them to a place of peace with me and with others. I call you my son, my child! You take after my own heart!

You are even blessed when others persecute you for acting in obedience to me. This is a small price to pay when you already possess my Kingdom and I promise you a great reward!

Dear child, I love to see you happy, enjoying all the blessings I have given you.

Matt. 5:1–10; John 15:9–11; 2 Sam. 22:28; John 1:16.

18

You Are My Witness

———— o ————

"Blessed are you when people insult you, persecute you and falsely say all kinds of evil against you because of me. Rejoice and be glad, because great is your reward in heaven."

(Matt. 5:11–12)

You have already discovered, beloved, that being my witness is sometimes costly. You can be misunderstood, persecuted, rejected and even hated. But the joy of belonging to my Kingdom far outweighs the cost, doesn't it? No matter what men do to you, **nobody can steal this Kingdom from you; you will never be deprived of your inheritance.**

You are blessed every time you suffer evil because of me. You tread the same path Jesus trod. You can be happy because your reward will be great in heaven. I reward faithfulness. Those who overcome will receive the crown of life; that is my promise.

You expect ridicule from unbelievers, but sometimes you have been surprised by the persecution from those who are faithful only to their religious philosophies and legalistic ideas. Don't fear such people and never compromise what you believe. Walk in the righteousness you know to be the truth, regardless of what anyone says to the contrary.

You are salt for the earth. Others can receive my life through you. They can see the example of godliness in you and benefit from my love that is evident in your life.

You are light for the world. My light dispels the darkness within you and can shine out of you. Don't hide this light. Don't be fearful or self-conscious about the way my light can be revealed through you. Others can benefit from what they see of me in you. Your example can even lead to them giving me glory.

Dear child, you are more conscious of the things about you that conceal rather than reveal Jesus; those things which need to be changed and don't glorify me. However, I assure you that **because my Spirit lives in you, Jesus is able to shine through your life, despite your failure and weakness.** Yes, others do see something of him in you. And so do I! And this causes me to rejoice! Yes, beloved, I rejoice over you with singing, and I have a rich reward awaiting you for all your faithful and loving obedience to me.

1 Pet. 1:3–6; Jas. 1:12; Matt. 5:13–16; 1 Pet. 4:16.

19

I AM

———— o ————

"I am in you."

(John 14:20)

Beloved, you live in me and I live in you. I revealed myself to Moses as "I am that I am". When Jesus came he used the phrase "I am" to reveal aspects of his ministry. In this way he revealed something of my own person and character. For whoever sees Jesus sees me; whoever knows him knows me; whoever loves him loves me.

Jesus said: **"I am the way, the truth and the life."** He is your way of salvation. He has revealed eternal truth through his words. He is your life.

Jesus said: **"I am the good shepherd."** He leads you in the paths of righteousness for my sake. He leads you to the rich pastures I want you to enjoy. Because you are one of my sheep you know his voice and are able to follow him.

Jesus said: **"I am the resurrection and the life."** Because you believe him you will not die eternally; you have received the gift of eternal life and he will raise you up at the last day.

Jesus said: **"I am the Alpha and Omega."** He is the beginning and the ending; the First and the Last; the

One who was and is and is to come. The Almighty One. And you live in him, child. You live in the Eternal, the Almighty One. And he lives in you!

Jesus said: **"I am the light of the world"** and he has already shone his light into your life.

Jesus said: **"I am with you always, to the very end of the age."** Rejoice in this wonderful truth, beloved child. He will always be with you.

Jesus said: **"I am the bread of life."** As you feed on his words, you feed on him. For his Spirit and life are in his words.

Jesus said: **"I am the living bread that came down from heaven."** Now he has returned to heaven and has taken you with him, beloved.

Jesus said: **"I am the gate for the sheep."** You have passed through that gate into my eternal life.

Jesus said: **"I am in the Father and the Father is in me."** This speaks of the unity of relationship we enjoy. Remember also, beloved child, that you are in him and he is in you; you are in me and I am in you. And this speaks of the unity we enjoy.

Jesus said: **"I am the true vine."** You are a branch in that vine, beloved disciple. Abide in the love of Jesus and you will bear much fruit.

There are so many wonderful truths for me to reveal to you!

John 14:6; John 10:11; John 11:25; Rev. 22:13; John 8:12; Matt 28:20; John 6:35; John 6:51; John 10:7; John 14:11; John 15:1.

20

I AM The Good Shepherd

——— o ———

"He calls his own sheep by name and leads them out."
(John 10:3)

I am the Good Shepherd. I want to lead you to rich pastures and show my loving care in the way I provide for you. In arid lands, sheep need to know the voice of the shepherd so they can follow him and find sufficient pasture. I don't leave you to your own devices, asking you to find your own pasture; I walk ahead of you in the way you are to go.

Beloved, I call you by name because you belong to me; you recognise my voice and follow me. I lead you beside still waters where you can know my peace, even in the midst of turmoil.

I have led you out of the dominion of darkness, out of Satan's grasp. I have led you out of condemnation and bondage. I have led you out from your past with all its sin and failure; and I have led you into my wonderful land of promise. That is where you are to live now.

It is never my purpose for you to starve spiritually. So don't look back. The one who does so is not fit for the Kingdom of heaven. Look forward. Reach out for what lies ahead of you. **You are able to participate in my divine nature through the very great and precious**

promises I have given you. You share in my life because of my love for you.

I have a pastor's heart, full of love for you. Only the hireling leaves the sheep in times of danger; but I have promised to be with you always. I will be a shield of protection about you. In me you will find your safety and security, and every need will be met as you believe my promises. You only have to trust in me!

Ps. 23; 2 Pet. 1:3–4; 2 Sam. 22:31.

21

Jesus Is The Gate

———— o ————

"I am the gate; whoever enters through me will be saved."

(John 10:9)

Jesus said, "I am the gate for the sheep." There is only one door which leads to life. Jesus! You have taken the only way to heaven! All other so-called "ways" seriously conflict with the truth.

There is only one truth and Jesus came to proclaim that truth. There is only one Saviour and he is that Saviour. There is only one sacrifice for sin and he is that sacrifice. There is only one Gate through which the sheep can pass. He is that Gate.

It saddens me that some hesitate to pass through because they think their unworthiness excludes them. I want to welcome them into my family, no matter how unworthy they have been. I have no desire to accuse them.

Some hesitate because they think I don't want them. Why should I provide this Gate if I didn't want people to pass through it into my Kingdom? Why should I provide a sacrifice for sin unless I wanted unworthy sinners to come to me? **The Gate is never slammed in the face of any who turn to me. I will not turn anyone away who comes to me through Jesus.**

Of course there are also others who don't want to pass through because they prefer to hold on to their life of sin. They realise that I require righteousness of my children. There are others who don't want to submit to my authority; they want to be their own lord and master.

And there are those who are too proud to pass through. They don't want to be dependent on anyone, and refuse to acknowledge their need even of me! Their intellect and natural ability are their gods. Well, I will never force them but I do invite them. You have discovered the eternal joy that lies beyond that Gate; so encourage others to pass through and know my love. Point them to Jesus. Assure them that they won't be rejected or turned away. A heavenly welcome awaits them. Be patient and persistent. Many need to hear the good news again and again before they respond and receive the life I want to give them. Was this true for you, beloved? If so, you will understand how patient and persistent I have to be.

John 10:7; John 6:37; Luke 15:7; Acts 4:12.

22

Ask

———— ○ ————

"Jesus said to her, 'Will you give me a drink?'"
(John 4:7)

It was a very hot day and Jesus had walked a great distance. He was thirsty and came to a well in Samaria. A local woman was drawing water, an odd thing to do at that time of day. He asked her for a drink.

The woman was surprised; it was unusual for a Jew to address a Samaritan and even more unusual for a man to address a woman in public. Jesus often did surprising things which challenged traditional practices!

Jesus wasn't ashamed to admit his need. His simple request opened the way for an encounter that changed not only the woman, but a whole village.

Often I ask you for a "drink", to do a simple thing for me. Sometimes you respond willingly; on other occasions you dismiss what I say. The request seemed too trivial and you couldn't foresee the immense fruit that would result from obedience. You failed to recognise who it was making the request, especially if spoken through someone else!

I want you to become increasingly sensitive to the voice of my Spirit and willing to obey me, even when I ask simple things of you. Prove faithful in small things.

Why should I expect you to do great things if you won't obey me in less important matters? And don't forget that your obedience may be a link in a chain of events I have planned that will bring blessing to many!

Learn this lesson well, beloved. **You only have to do what I tell you and then leave the outcome to me.**

Don't limit me by your reason! And don't imagine you know my business better than I do! If you realise that obedience will cause certain shock-waves, know that I am even more aware of that than you. I judge those repercussions to be beneficial, even if uncomfortable. Sometimes you are concerned about the way others will judge you for your obedience. This is the cause of your hesitancy, isn't it, child?

Peter was concerned when told to visit Cornelius. His obedience led to the salvation of many, although the vision I gave him indicated that he would have to break with tradition and he knew others would criticise him for that.

Jesus broke with tradition; so did Peter and so will you, if you are to be obedient to me. So, beloved, listen to what I say and do it.

John 4:7–26; Matt. 25:21; John 10:3–5.

23

Have Compassion

———— o ————

"When he saw the crowds, he had compassion on them, because they were harassed and helpless, like sheep without a shepherd."

(Matt. 9:36)

N otice how gentle Jesus was with the woman at the well. She was in the grip of sin and he wanted to save her. The way to her heart was not through words of accusation; he offered her the living water of salvation. Only that would satisfy her spiritual need.

The woman sensed his love, not the kind of love to which she was accustomed, but genuine concern for her as a person. Throughout her life of sin, she had looked for love and acceptance, for someone to value her for herself. She needed forgiveness, to be cleansed from the guilt of former years and all her futile relationships.

She could only give Jesus a cup of ordinary water. He gave her the living water of eternal life. But she gave first! Beloved, **have you noticed how often you receive only when you have first given?** What I ask you to give will be nothing in comparison to what I give you in return. Nevertheless this is the right order; **you give and then I give to you.**

You cannot buy my blessings with a "cup of water". But your willingness to give, and to ask for what you need, opens the way for me to give to you and enables you to receive.

Don't judge those you serve in my name; reach out with my mercy and compassion. Don't be afraid to ask for their help; don't be too proud to receive from them. This can open the way for you to help them. They may give you a glass of water; you can show them how to receive eternal life.

My Spirit can show you the need in a person's life. Lovingly and sensitively you can speak into that need, showing how much I care. Don't be put off if people reject what you say or the love you offer. I am often rejected.

Matt. 9:35–8; John 4:4–26; Col. 4:5; 2 Cor. 9:6–11.

24

Come To Me!

———— ∘ ————

**"Come to me, all you who are weary and burdened . . .
and you will find rest for your souls."**

(Matt. 11:28–9)

I see the poor, the destitute, and I invite them to come
to me. I see all those who feel they cannot cope with
the demands of life, those weighed down by oppression. I tell them to come to me.

I see those who have experienced opposition, hurt,
rejection and neglect; and I invite them to come to me.

I see those who think of themselves as complete failures, useless rejects; I want them to come to me.

I see the wealthy who have tried to use their riches
to acquire happiness and satisfaction, yet within them
there is a sense of futility and emptiness. I call them to
come to me.

I see those for whom life is drudgery, a ceaseless
round of hard work with little reward, and I invite them
to come to me.

I see those with meagre resources who can scarcely
provide for their families. I see those who feel they are
not gifted at anything or special in any way; those who
have no sense of an ultimate meaning to their life or of

their personal worth, and I say to all of them: "Come to me!"

I see the sick, those whose bodies and emotions are wrecked by pain; I want them to come to me.

I see those in positions of power and authority, some careful in the fulfilling of their responsibilities, others corrupt; and I command them to come to me.

Some don't hear my voice; often others don't want to hear. Many are called, but few are chosen. My gospel is good news for all; I alone can answer their needs.

I see those who follow other religions. Some are proud, others are deceived by these ideologies and philosophies. I want them to know the truth because only the truth will set them free from their sin and bondage. I see how the god of this age has blinded the minds of unbelievers and I am angry. That blindness deprives many of my love.

What do you see, beloved? Do you see what I see? Do you have the same compassion for the lost in your heart as I have in mine?

Please tell others that I want them to come to me and receive my life. I will not turn away any who do.

Matt. 11:25–30; Isa. 55:1–3; Matt. 22:14; 2 Cor. 4:4.

25

Admit Your Need

———— o ————

"He who did not spare his own Son, but gave him up for us all – how will he not also, along with him, graciously give us all things?"

(Rom. 8:32)

Beloved, never be ashamed to admit your need. Don't be afraid to ask someone to help you. Don't stand on your pride. Sometimes you have been too "spiritual", unwilling to make your need known or ask for help. You have justified this by saying you trust the Lord!

I rejoice that you trust me. However, sometimes you have failed to realise that **I have arranged for the right person to be in the right place at the right time for your benefit!** If you had been humble enough to ask for help, the need would have been met! There is little point in saying you trust me and then refusing the way I choose to answer you! I know you don't like to receive from others because then you feel indebted to them. It also strains at your love of independence, doesn't it?

Beloved, I am active in the details of your life. People don't cross your path by accident!

Your failure to ask deprives others of the joy of giving to you, and the blessing they will receive as a result. Think of your pleasure and satisfaction when you have served and blessed others! What confusion there would be if everyone wanted to give but no one wanted to receive from others!

At other times you have not brought your need to me, thinking it too trivial a matter to concern your God. "You do not receive because you do not ask." There have been many occasions when I would willingly have given to you if only you had asked. It is no trouble to me to bless you in whatever way is needed, in small or truly significant matters. I have given you so much already as proof of that.

Consider this, beloved; does a father only give to his child when the need is great? Does he not care for him daily in the small details as well as the major concerns? Well, I am your Father and that is how I care for you!

Matt. 7:7–8; Jas. 4:2; 2 Cor. 8:14–15.

26

The Joy of Sharing

———— o ————

"I am willing," he said. "Be clean!"

(Matt. 8:3)

The needy clung to Jesus' words. They saw in him one who could meet their needs.

leper came tentatively saying, "If you are willing, you can make me clean." Jesus told him, "I am willing," and spoke the word of authority that set him free: "Be clean." Immediately his leprosy left him.

The leper came unsure of Jesus' love for him. He came with an "if". Jesus simply removed the "if"!

Beloved, come to me boldly. Don't think that I love others but not you. Because I love you I want to give to you. I am willing to heal you and meet your need. **You don't need to come to me with an "if"!** "If you are willing," or "If it is your will."

When Jesus healed people, or delivered them from demonic forces, they were filled with joy and gratitude. It is the same today. When my power touches lives people are thankful. The praise which comes from their hearts blesses me. Would you continue to give to those who are ungrateful and show no gratitude?

What contrast in the attitudes of those who opposed Jesus because of the hardness of their hearts! They were more concerned about their religious rules than the welfare of the people. Jesus didn't come with rules and regulations, but with life!

His opponents saw in those who flocked to Jesus a joy they did not have themselves, for all their learning and knowledge of the law. Instead of coming to the source of that joy, they bitterly resented him for his popularity and effectiveness in meeting people's needs.

There are still many like that today. They perform no miracles themselves, but hinder those who turn to me in their need. Their religious traditions are powerless and ineffective.

Don't be like that, child. **Rejoice and be glad when you see others receiving from me.** Be pleased for them, but also recognise that they could only receive what I had chosen to give.

There is no need for you to be jealous. You, too, are my child; it gives me joy to bless you by meeting your need. And I rejoice when you receive gladly from me. **I am blessed every time I give, and you are blessed every time you receive.**

Matt. 8:1–4; Heb. 10:19–23; Heb. 4:16; Rom. 2:11; Matt. 10:8; Heb. 6:10.

27

The Faith Of A Centurion

———— o ————

"But say the word, and my servant will be healed."
(Luke 7:7)

My dear child, this is the kind of faith that I want you to have! The centurion came to Jesus with the simple trust that he would heal his servant. When Jesus offered to come to his house, the centurion recognised that he didn't deserve such a privilege. Jesus only had to give the command and his servant would be healed.

Here was someone who understood authority. The centurion knew what it was to give orders and to obey them. He recognised that Jesus had supreme authority; he only had to speak and the healing would be effected from a distance!

No wonder Jesus was surprised. This Gentile had more understanding of his authority than any Jew, including his own disciples! He exhibited a faith beyond any of them!

Do you not see, child, that the one with faith in me recognises the authority with which I speak? He doesn't argue with my words; he believes them. He knows I only have to give the command and the sick are healed, the blind see, the crippled walk and even the dead are raised to life. More than that, **HE EXPECTS ME TO**

GIVE THE ORDER. Yes, he comes to me with that expectation. **He not only knows I can; he expects I will.**

It is that kind of expectant faith that I want you to have, child. To me this is not presumption; it is obedience to my word, recognition of my authority and trust in my promises.

His listeners were surprised and even upset when Jesus said that people would come from other nations to share in my heavenly feast; while those to whom I came would find themselves shut out because of their unbelief.

Jesus told the servant it would be done exactly as he believed. That is still my word, child. It is my word to you today and every day. **It will be done for you just as you believed. That is the power of faith in my authority – and my love!**

Luke 7:1–10; Heb. 10:22; Heb. 4:16; Matt. 10:8; 1 John 5:14–15.

28

My Healing Touch

———— ○ ————

"When evening came, many who were demon-possessed were brought to him, and he drove out the spirits with a word and healed all the sick. This was to fulfil what was spoken through the prophet Isaiah: 'He took up our infirmities and carried our diseases.'"
(Matt. 8:16–17)

I love to heal people. Every act of healing is an evidence of my mercy and tender love. I am full of compassion for those in need and I expressed this in the way Jesus healed people and set them free.

Compassion is more than concern. Jesus was not content to be sorry for people; neither did he merely support them in their need. Because he had compassion he healed them, liberating the captives, setting people free. Such actions expressed the love in my heart.

Whenever there was faith in Jesus nothing could withstand his authority. Where there was unbelief, as at Nazareth, even Jesus could not heal many. That demonstrates the power of faith and the negative effect of unbelief.

Jesus ensured that his power to heal was not confined to the generation in which he lived on earth. When he went to the cross he took on himself the sin of all mankind of every generation. **He also carried all their sicknesses and infirmities. He overcame every spiritual power of darkness. What he had done for one generation through his ministry became available to every generation.**

So whatever he said and did in that generation applies today. Whenever faith operates it is as if you live in Bible times; you experience healings and miracles taking place. Jesus is the same yesterday, today and for ever. Unbelief, more than anything else, hinders my healing purposes.

You can understand why I rejoice in the faith of my children for it demonstrates my purpose has not changed. It is still my will to heal. **This is still the commission I have given my Church: heal the sick.** I still expect this command to be obeyed.

I rejoice, child, whenever you believe me to meet a need in your own life, and when you encourage faith in others by sharing my word with them. Don't be put off by those who oppose my healing purposes through their unbelief and misunderstanding of my word. Persevere in your faith, believing the truth of my word.

Isa. 53:5; Mark 16:17–20; Jas. 5:14–15.

29

The Ruler's Daughter Raised

———— o ————

"He went in and took the girl by the hand, and she got up."

(Matt. 9:25)

First Jesus cleared the mourners out of the room. It is a spiritual principle to clear unbelief out of the way so that faith can operate.

Those who had their eyes set on the problem laughed at Jesus. How could anyone raise this child from the dead? For Jesus, it was a simple matter. He went into the room where she lay, took her by the hand saying: "Little girl, I say to you, get up." And she stood up and walked around.

To the onlookers she was dead. To Jesus she was merely asleep. **Unbelief and faith have entirely different perspectives on the same event or set of circumstances. Unbelief accepts the situation as it is. Faith sees what shall be as if it is!**

Jesus was prepared to speak his faith in the midst of unbelief, even though he was ridiculed as a result: "The child is not dead but asleep."

When you speak in faith you will often be ridiculed by others who don't see what you see. Don't allow this to deter you, child. Was she dead? Oh yes! When Jesus told her to get up her spirit returned.

Can you raise the dead? Yes. But I am not telling you to go to the local mortuary and try your hand! Remember, Jesus did only what he saw me doing, and he spoke only the words I gave him to speak. You will need to listen to the voice of my Spirit and be led by him.

Sometimes my children say: "I am going to believe God to do it." They are usually disappointed at the results. Such an attitude is not faith operating. Faith comes from hearing; it is a response to my word.

There will be many situations in which I speak a word of faith to you in the face of what seem impossible odds. People will laugh at you for believing what I say rather than accepting the circumstances. Never mind the laughter. **What I have said, I have said. What I have promised shall surely come to pass.**

So hold on to my words, beloved. Don't lose sight of them. **Speak your faith openly and decisively, no matter what reaction you receive from others.** And you will see that what I have promised shall surely come to pass.

Matt. 9:18–26; Heb. 11:1; John 8:28; Ps. 145:13; 2 Cor. 4:13.

30

I Honour Faith

———— o ————

"'Yes, Lord,' she replied, 'but even the dogs under the table eat the children's crumbs.'"

(Mark 7:28)

It sometimes perplexes people as to why non-believers can be healed when many who believe in me are not healed.

Jesus knew his mission was to the lost people of Israel. He had to give opportunity first to my covenant people to repent and believe the good news. The time would come when the gospel would be made available to all nations, but Jesus had to go first to the Jews and then the truth would be taken to the Gentiles.

This Gentile woman had real faith. **I will never deny faith in me. I will always answer the prayer of faith. I stand by my word and promises and will never contradict them.** This woman demonstrated faith by saying that even the dogs ate the crumbs that fell from the rich man's table. Just a crumb of what I could give her would be enough to effect the deliverance of her daughter. I had to honour such faith.

I taught my disciples that if they had faith the size of a seed they would be able to cast mountains into the sea, and speak to a tree and see it moved from one place to another. It is the quality of faith that counts. You don't need a great deal of faith but the simple trust that I will do what I have said I will do. You only have to believe me. I love to see faith demonstrated in you. Listen to what Jesus said to the woman: "First let the children eat as much as they want." Are you not my child? This means you don't have to scratch around on the floor under the table looking for crumbs. **I have given you a place at the table. You can eat as much as you want.**

If a crumb effects such a healing, what could the entire feast do for you? You only have to come with faith to the table of my provision.

Beloved, don't hold back wondering whether it could really be true that I want you sitting with me. **You have your place at my table. Come with a sincere heart and in full assurance of faith!**

Mark 7:24–30; Rom. 1:16; Matt. 17:20–1; Luke 17:6; Heb. 10:22.

31

I Lead You

———— ∘ ————

"Return home and tell how much God has done for you."

(Luke 8:39)

J esus' food was to do my will and to finish the work I gave him. He fulfilled everything I asked of him. He was only interested in doing my will and purpose. **He had no plans of his own. He lived in constant submission to my will, attentive to the voice of my Holy Spirit.** He went where I led him and did what I told him. His encounters with different people were part of my plan for his ministry. He made sure he was at the right place at the right time.

Jesus crossed the Sea of Galilee to free a demon-possessed man called Legion because so many demons lived in him. It was worth making such a journey for this one encounter.

The man was so grateful for his deliverance, he wanted to follow Jesus. Instead he was told to tell others what had been done for him. You see, one encounter could lead to a whole area being reached with the gospel. The complete transformation of his life was a witness to all who knew him. I often choose the toughest cases, to use the most unlikely people.

To some it would seem a waste of time to go all that

way to minister to one man; but that was my will. Jesus didn't argue; he did what I said. And what joy to see that man set free!

If you are sensitive to the voice of my Spirit, he will lead you in the same way. You will be at the right place at the right time. **What seem like chance encounters to you, are often carefully planned by me!**

You are sometimes the one I have chosen to bring my answer to another. I send you to others with my love, compassion and forgiveness. You go in my name, with my authority.

So don't listen to the voice of doubt. I want to use you, beloved. I use all who are prepared to reach out to others in my name.

Luke 8:26–39; John 12:49–50; John 6:38; Ps. 139:16; Eph. 2:10.

32

The Storm

———— ◦ ————

"Where is your faith?"

(Luke 8:25)

A t times you have allowed difficult circumstances to prevent you from doing what I asked!

As Jesus crossed the Lake to meet Legion, he slept in the stern of the boat. A sudden storm arose and his disciples were very afraid, even though some were experienced fishermen. They decided to wake Jesus.

Imagine crossing the sea with Jesus and thinking they could be drowned! They were like you, weren't they? There have been many times when you have been fearful, even though I have been with you!

Jesus stood up and rebuked the wind and waves. Immediately there was a great calm. The disciples were amazed that he should have such authority. "Where is your faith?" he asked them.

Do you understand what was happening? Jesus was on his way to free a demon-possessed man. When my Spirit leads you to do something that will inflict specific defeat on the enemy, adverse circumstances can try to hinder you. Don't be deterred. **As you obey the leading of my Spirit you can overcome those hindrances.** Don't give in to them and turn back.

When Moses sent twelve men to spy out the promised land, only two returned with a positive attitude. The rest thought the hindrances too great to see my word fulfilled. They believed the circumstances that confronted them rather than the promises I had given.

When you are about my business don't allow anything to stand in your way, either natural circumstances or hindrances contrived by the enemy. **You have authority to overcome in my name.** Finish the task and don't allow anything to deter you.

If you submit yourself to my will and resist the enemy, he will flee from you. He has no right to prevent you from doing what I want.

It's a question of faith, isn't it, child? Jesus made that clear. Stand in faith against every adverse circumstance. The testing of your faith proves that it is genuine.

Luke 8:22–5; 1 John 5:4–5; 1 Pet. 1:7; Rom. 8:31,35–7.

33

According to Your Faith

——— o ———

"What do you want me to do for you?"

(Mark 10:51)

Bartimaeus, the blind beggar at Jericho, cried out to Jesus: "Son of David! Have mercy on me!" Those around him tried to silence him. Why should Jesus be concerned with the likes of him?

"What do you want me to do for you?" Jesus asked him. "I want my sight back," he replied. That simple answer revealed that he believed Jesus would heal him.

"According to your faith it will be done to you," Jesus said.

This is still my word to all people of every generation. It is my word to you, beloved: **According to your faith it will be done to you.** My mercy, grace, love and power are the same today as they were then.

My love for you is as great as my love for Bartimaeus. Don't be afraid to cry out to me as he did. And don't be put off by others' views. You can come directly to me. You believe I am your Saviour and Lord. You believe I am your Father who loves you. Do you believe I am your healer?

Sadly, not all my children believe I want to heal them. Some even suggest I want them to be sick. If this is the case, why do they do everything they can to get better? You can see, child, the inconsistency in such attitudes. This is double-mindedness.

Still others believe I use sickness to refine and train my children. What kind of father would that make me? How could I claim to be faithful to my new covenant of love if I treated my children like that?

Certainly I am able to use every situation in positive and creative ways. I don't condemn my children for being sick. I continue to love and encourage them. I speak to them, change and comfort them. But I do all these things in times of health as well as in times of sickness. I don't need to make my children sick in order to work within them!

So be single-minded about my desire to heal my people. This is why Jesus took all your infirmities upon himself when he went to the cross. Don't accept sickness as my will for you. Learn to resist this together with all other forces of evil.

Beloved, keep praying for others and ministering to them. Know that I am blessed by every healing that takes place.

Mark 10:46–52; 1 John 5:14–15; Eph. 3:12; Isa. 53:4–5.

34

Touch Me With Faith

———— ∘ ————

"If I only touch his cloak, I will be healed."
(Matt. 9:21)

T he woman with the haemorrhage was determined. She pressed through the crowds to touch Jesus. Immediately power went out of him because he had been touched by faith!

I am touched by faith, when my children pray with faith; in response I answer with my power. The woman thought Jesus would be displeased with her, but he loved the boldness and determination of genuine faith that she displayed.

I long to see such faith in my children today. People cannot touch me physically; but they can touch me with their faith. I am more accessible to you now than Jesus was to that woman. You don't have to come through a crowd to one particular place where I am present. I am with you always. Everything that hinders you can be overcome by the blood of Jesus and the word of your testimony.

Do you understand what this means? In the sacrifice of Jesus I have overcome all sin and sorrow, all sickness and infirmity, all oppression and evil. **You have available to you everything that is accomplished through the shedding of that innocent blood.**

You don't have to ask me to do what I have already done. By faith take hold of the victory Jesus has already won for you.

If you do that, you will speak accordingly – not of the problem, but of the solution; not of the need, but of the promises; not of the sickness, but of the healing; not of the sin, but of my mercy. Your words of testimony will affirm that you believe the victory and are one who overcomes.

Beloved child, **touch me with faith and I assure you that power will go out from me and into your life every time you do so.**

Matt. 9:20–2; Rev. 12:11; Isa. 53:4–5; 1 John 5:4–5.

35

Forgiven and Healed

———— o ————

"'But that you may know that the Son of Man has authority on earth to forgive sins . . .' He said to the paralysed man, 'I tell you, get up, take your mat and go home.'"

(Luke 5:24)

I love to see practical faith operating in the lives of my people. Those who brought the paralysed man to Jesus couldn't get near him because of the crowd. So they opened the roof and lowered the man in front of Jesus. Such an action was a demonstration of their faith.

They believed they only had to bring their friend to Jesus and he would be healed. They were so determined they wouldn't allow any adverse circumstances to deter them. This is an example for you to follow. I like to see such determination in the way you act.

When faith operates in your heart, nothing prevents you from holding on with perseverance to the word I have spoken to you until you see the outcome I have promised.

Jesus forgave the paralysed man; this was his greatest need. Sin can cause sickness. It can also prevent people from receiving healing.

The religious leaders considered it blasphemy for Jesus to forgive sins. They knew that I alone could forgive. If Jesus had been given such authority he must be acting in my name. They didn't want to acknowledge this, and so to submit to him; for such submission would involve many changes in their lives. Like many religious people, they had no intention of changing their ways. They wanted people to recognise them, to respect their religious authority and positions. Because Jesus threatened them with his greater spiritual authority, they hated him and plotted to kill him. Such religious attitudes are always in opposition to true faith.

Sometimes you will find that other people, especially religious ones, will not like the authority you exercise. They will be jealous of your certainty of faith and will think you foolish for holding on to the promises I have given you. They will encourage you to believe the circumstances rather than my word, to believe what you see with your eyes rather than what you hear with your heart. They will want you to respect the positions of men rather than the authority of my words. Such authoritarianism has never healed anyone!

Jesus showed his true spiritual authority by forgiving and then healing the man. He needed only a few words to do so.

Beloved, I rejoice when you trust in my authority, when you receive the word I speak to you with faith. But don't be surprised when "religious" people oppose you! They oppose me too! They even crucified my Son!

Luke 5:17–26; Rom. 4:18–21; 2 Pet. 1:3–4; Col. 2:8; Mark 7:1–13.

36

Your Assurance

―――― ० ――――

"For my Father's will is that everyone who looks to the Son and believes in him shall have eternal life, and I will raise him up at the last day."

(John 6:40)

I not only heal the sick; I raise the dead. **The power of my eternal Kingdom is greater than death.**

Jesus loved Lazarus dearly. When Jesus heard of his sickness he proclaimed immediately, "This sickness will not end in death." The enemy would not triumph in this situation. Do you realise that Jesus was speaking words of faith? He didn't go rushing to the scene in a frenzy of unbelief, but had the assurance that Lazarus would be raised. **He spoke what he believed into being.**

Two days later he set out for Bethany with his disciples. "I am going there to wake him up," he said. **Again he was speaking faith.** Both Mary and Martha believed his death could have been prevented if only Jesus had been present. He hadn't come to mourn a lost friend, but to raise him. He commanded that the stone in front of the tomb be moved. To the women he said: "Did I not tell you that if you believed, you would see the glory of God?"

Jesus prayed with faith in front of the tomb: **"Father, I thank you that you have heard me. I know that you**

always hear me." Yes, I had heard every word Jesus had uttered about the situation. And every word, *no matter to whom it was spoken*, was a positive affirmation of faith.

Jesus cried out loudly, "Lazarus, come out!" He spoke to the "mountain" of need. Lazarus came out of the tomb, bound in his grave clothes. The people were awe-struck. **Notice that he thanked me before anything had happened. That is faith.**

Notice, child, the consistency with which Jesus spoke faith in this situation, whether speaking to me or to others. Often my children say one thing in prayer to me, then contradict this by what they say in conversation to others. Faith is an attitude of heart, and Jesus did not waver in his faith!

Jesus raised not only Lazarus but also the widow's son and the synagogue ruler's daughter. Some are raised from the dead today, when there is faith in the hearts of my people to believe for such a miracle. I am the Author of such faith!

However, those who believe in me don't need to fear death; it is but the gateway to glory!

At the last day, Jesus will raise all those who put their trust and confidence in him. As you believe in him, your resurrection is assured and you have my eternal life within you already.

John 6:36–40; John 11:1–44; Heb. 12:2; 1 Cor. 15:54–5.

37

I Heal You

———— o ————

"Surely he took up our infirmities . . . and by his wounds we are healed."

(Isa. 53:4–5)

What Jesus had to endure to make it possible for you to receive healing was costly. Lashes were applied to his body one after another. Every one of them meant healing for my children. The pain he bore in righteousness, he suffered for the pain of the unrighteous. He never sinned, yet took all sin on himself. He was never sick but took all sickness on himself.

The prophet foretold that the Messiah would bear the infirmities of the people and by the stripes laid on him they would be healed.

He came to bring health of spirit, soul and body. Through the activity of my Spirit, people are born again and transformed into my likeness. By that same mighty power sicknesses are healed. And by that same power the dead are raised.

Beloved, because I have the ability to do such things I can certainly meet every need in your life. I am able to do far more than you can ask or imagine, **according to the power of my Spirit that is at work within you.**

It is mystifying that many subscribe to the fact that Jesus healed throughout his ministry, but they don't expect him to heal today. Those same people expect to be raised from the dead by the power of my Spirit. They think some of my divine power and glory has been lost, or no longer functions. Once Jesus saved, healed and raised from the dead. Now they say he saves and raises, but no longer heals! That is unbelief.

I taught you to pray that my Kingdom will come on earth as it is in heaven. There is no sickness in heaven. All sorrow and tears have passed away. **If there is no sickness in heaven it is my will that there should be no sickness on earth.**

No matter what your need, it is my purpose to heal you. My healing power is always available to you. Exercise your faith and receive all that Jesus died to give you. Come to me and receive my healing.

Is your need too great for me? Do you look at twisted limbs and maimed bodies and say that such healings are impossible? Only the limitations of your faith confine me.

"Who has believed our message and to whom has the arm of the Lord been revealed?"

Isa. 53:4–5; Eph. 3:20; 2 Cor. 5:21; Matt. 21:22.

38

Speak Out Faith

———— o ————

"If you have faith as small as a mustard seed, you can say to this mountain, 'Move from here to there' and it will move. Nothing will be impossible for you."

(Matt. 17:20)

Like Jesus you will have to speak to situations as well as to me. **You need to speak in faith, with authority, determined that what you say shall surely happen.** When you speak to mountains of need, command them to be moved. Don't doubt in your heart, but believe.

Many fall into the trap of speaking about their need instead of speaking against it with faith and authority. To speak about the need makes the situation worse because you are affirming the problem. Speak against it in my name; command it to be moved.

Your words have great power – for good or evil. They can bring you into liberty or condemnation, truth or error, healing or sickness.

Often your words are spoken out of fear and anxiety instead of faith, especially where sickness and need are concerned. Fear is a tool of the enemy. He wants you to concentrate on the sickness rather than the Healer. Learn to resist him.

Remember, there is to be a consistency about what you say to me, to others and to the situation itself. From the overflow of faith in your heart your mouth will speak faith. Only if you are double-minded will you say one thing and then readily change your mind. A double-minded man cannot expect to receive the answer from me; he doesn't know what he believes himself!

When you first experience a symptom, do you start to worry or do you speak to it in my name, commanding it to go? Use your faith and authority to resist attacks of sickness.

Dear child, what you say about your circumstances must agree with what you pray about your circumstances. And what you pray needs to agree with what I say. Then you can both pray and speak with the utmost confidence.

Matt. 17:19–20; Luke 6:45; 1 John 5:14–15; Jas. 1:6–8.

39

The Power of Your Words

———— o ————

"With the tongue we praise our Lord and Father, and with it we curse men . . . My brothers, this should not be."

(Jas. 3:9–10)

Beloved, use your spiritual authority. Why do you think I have given it to you?

After Jesus had cursed the fig tree, the disciples were amazed to discover on the following day that it had already withered. Why the surprise? Whatever Jesus blessed was blessed; whatever he cursed was cursed. He always spoke with my authority.

You can speak blessing or curse. You have authority to speak and pray in the name of Jesus. Whatever you speak has a profound effect on what happens, whether you realise this or not.

You are learning to speak blessing, healing and deliverance to people. But you can also speak criticism, failure, judgment, condemnation – even curses! **Realise the power in everything you say, either for good or bad.**

I want you to speak in faith, not fear; blessing, not curse! **The more of my authority you exercise in the way you speak, the more my power can be released**

into a situation. You have authority to bring whatever you say into being.

If you speak wrongly about yourself, you place your life under those words. Many people curse themselves by the things they say about themselves, instead of agreeing with what my word says about them. They need to repent.

On the day of judgment all will have to give account for every careless word they have spoken. **Understand the power of your words, the importance of everything you say.**

Jesus spoke curses only when he intended to. He spoke judgment only when necessary. He spoke correction only in love. He didn't speak negatively or flippantly about people behind their backs. His purpose was to bless at all times. That is your purpose too, isn't it? You want to bring blessing on yourself and to others. **So realise the impact of your words both on your own life and others to whom you speak.**

Dear child, your tongue is like a rudder that steers the course of a ship. Steer your life in the way of my word, for whenever your speech contradicts my word, you steer off-course; you depart from my intended purpose for you. **Agree with my words, for it is the renewing of your mind which will bring the transformation in your life that both you and I want to see! Let your thinking agree with my word, beloved.**

Jas. 3:3–12; Matt 21:18–22; Rom. 12:14; Matt. 12:34–7; 1 Pet. 4:11; Rom. 12:2.

40

So Shall It Be!

—— o ——

"But say the word, and my servant will be healed."
(Luke 7:7)

Whatever I speak into your life will surely happen. I may speak directly through my word or by my Spirit. I may use someone else as my mouthpiece. It is not the voice that matters, but the word that I speak to you.

What do you expect me to say? Do you want me to commiserate with you over the sickness? Are you looking for explanations as to why you have certain symptoms? Do you want to know the reasons why there is sickness in your body or soul? Will it really help you if you know all these things? Is that how I approached the needs of people when Jesus walked on earth?

No, he didn't go into detailed analysis of the situation. He simply spoke the word of command and they were healed. Isn't that what you want – the healing? That simple word of authority that will bring you release and healing? I am certainly willing to speak that word. Are you able to receive it?

Jesus said: **"As you believe, so let it be." "According to your faith let it be done to you."**

The principle still applies today. Do you believe that I will speak the word of power and authority to your heart, and that whatever I speak will surely be performed? Is this too simple for you? Too direct and forthright? Are you looking instead to men or to methods? Do you believe the authority of my word? Are you listening for the voice of my Spirit?

I use men, but I will never be limited by their methods. My Spirit blows wherever he wills and he is already blowing through your life, beloved. Believe the words he speaks to you. For truly, as you believe, so shall it be!

Luke 7:1–10; Matt. 9:29; Matt. 8:13; John 3:8.

41

Be Healed!

———— o ————

"I am the Lord, who heals you."

(Ex. 15:26)

"**D**on't be afraid; just believe."

"Be opened."

"Rise and walk."

"Your faith has healed you."

Beloved, receive my healing. I tell you clearly, **"I am willing."** I love you and touch your life with my love. This is the work of my grace for which you have longed. You have waited; now you can receive. My Spirit is at work in you even now. I speak my word of command. Sickness leaves your body. Healing life flows into you at this moment. Be healed in my name, for my glory.

Mark 5:36; Mark 10:52.

42

One Step of Faith

——— o ———

"Then Peter got down out of the boat, walked on the water and came towards Jesus."

(Matt. 14:29)

When Jesus called Peter, he knew him to be an impetuous man. But he was big-hearted and a natural leader. He possessed great potential. He was willing to step out in faith and was not afraid to make mistakes; neither was he deterred by his failures.

Peter walked on water! He was the only one who had the boldness to step out of the security of the boat. Jesus chided him for his lack of faith when he began to sink. He started with faith and would have continued to walk on the water if he had been steadfast in faith, instead of being distracted by the wind and waves. He was learning that there are no limits to what can be done through faith in me.

Do you ever limit me, child?

Peter was the first to recognise Jesus as my Son. Yet at first he could not accept what Jesus prophesied concerning his suffering and crucifixion. Instead, he listened to the voice of reason which often contradicts the truth.

From that experience he learned another important lesson. One moment he could be used as my mouthpiece; the next he spoke as the enemy who opposes the truth.

Do you ever oppose my truth because you listen to your reason instead? Do you begin with faith, then believe the situation?

When all his disciples deserted Jesus at the time of his arrest, Peter did at least follow him. He had been so certain that he would not fail Jesus. Yet, even after deserting him, he denied him three times.

But Jesus didn't condemn him. He looked at him with compassion, not judgment.

You have denied me sometimes, haven't you, beloved? And you have been afraid to step out of the boat. There have been occasions when you began with faith but then took your eyes off me. There have been times when you have spoken my words; then have contradicted the truth.

Peter's failures are recorded in scripture for your benefit. **Realise that I don't condemn you or cut you off from fellowship with me because you fail.** My purpose is to forgive, accept and restore you.

The sight of Jesus in his risen body washed away Peter's feelings of fear and frustration with himself. It's the same for you, isn't it? One encounter with me frees you from any sense of failure. You realise I have been with you, even during the times when you failed to trust me. Things have gone wrong as a result, but I have never deserted you. I have waited for you to turn to me for help or forgiveness.

Don't condemn yourself to a life where failure is your expectation.

Notice the changes that took place when Peter was filled with the Holy Spirit. He became bold and confident in proclaiming the truth. I used him to perform mighty miracles. He stood up to the authorities that opposed him. He still made mistakes; he compromised and Paul had to correct him. But he obeyed when I sent him to Cornelius. He had learned to obey me rather than listen to his own reason.

Each of my disciples undergoes a training programme which I supervise personally. You have received a faith as precious as that of Peter and the other apostles. Such faith is in you. As you put your trust in my word you will have a far greater confidence than you have demonstrated in the past. You will not be so impetuous, or so easily downcast because of difficult circumstances or opposition. Like Peter in prison, you will trust me in the midst of the problems and see my deliverance again and again.

Identify with the triumphs as well as the failures of these men. The same Spirit who lived in them lives in you.

Matt. 14:25–32; Matt. 16:21–3; John 21:15–19; Acts 3: 1–16; 2 Pet. 1:1; Ps. 34:19.

43

I Love You

———— o ————

**"You are precious and honoured in my sight, and . . .
I love you."**

(Isa. 43:4)

Because I love you I sent Jesus to die for **you**. Because
I love you I will raise you to my eternal glory.
Because I love you I want you for ever.

Please don't doubt my love, beloved. You are forgiven
and accepted. There is no need to fear the demands I
make on you. You are not a failure; you are my child.

All Jesus' disciples made mistakes; yet all were
restored, except the one who had to be lost. You are not
a Judas! Unlike him you have received my Spirit, the
guarantee that you are mine and have an eternal
inheritance.

I want the very best for you. Second best is not good
enough for you because you are mine! I have a plan for
your life just as I had a plan for Jesus. I don't hide from
you that at times it will prove costly. It will require
the dedication of your whole life. You are to love me
wholeheartedly, holding nothing back. What does the
cost matter when compared with the benefits?

You are yoked with me. My yoke is easy. My burden
is light. Do you understand what I am saying? Even

when the pressures and demands seem more than you can bear, I will carry the burden because you are yoked with me. I will take the weight. It doesn't matter how much you put on my shoulders, you can never weigh me down. You can even place yourself on my shoulders and I will carry you.

Dear child, there will be times when it seems you cannot walk because you lack the strength. You cannot see your way through the predicament that faces you. **I promise to carry you.** Don't be like a child who refuses to be carried. Don't try to be independent. Let me lift you in my everlasting arms. I shelter you under the shadow of my wings. I gather you to myself. **Because I love you, I want you close to me.** Don't be afraid to draw near to me. I will always be waiting for you.

Rom. 5:8; 1 John 3:1; Eph. 1:13–14; Matt. 11:28–30; Isa. 43:1–7; Isa. 40:11; Isa. 41:9–10.

44

I Heal The Broken-Hearted

———— o ————

"He heals the broken-hearted and binds up their wounds."

(Ps. 147:3)

Beloved child, it seemed that you were deprived suddenly of one who was so precious to you. I could see that you felt heart-broken. I saw your tears; I knew your feelings of emptiness. I heard your cry of "Why? Why?"

For a time your grief seemed to separate you from me, didn't it? Then you discovered me in the grief. Yes, I was with you still, even though you couldn't understand what was happening. You clung on to my words of promise by your fingertips, didn't you?

And then you began to discover how I heal the broken-hearted. Self-pity didn't help, did it? That only confused the issue. For a time you wondered what possible purpose your life could hold now. Life suddenly seemed so fragile, didn't it? Do you remember that moment when it seemed that you hung on to life by only a thread? You thought it would be easier for the thread to be cut, and everything to end.

But I brought you through that time, didn't I? I provided people to comfort you, although you thought that no one could really understand what you were going through. **What mattered most was that you came to realise that I understood, that I cared, that I alone could fill that emptiness, that only I could heal the wound you felt deep inside.**

And so the healing has been taking place within you. **The most significant moment was when you stopped looking back and began to look forward. It was at that point that your self-pity gave way to faith again.**

See how I sustained you when you thought it was impossible for faith to operate in you. I brought you back to the place of trusting. Now you realise that your life is not over, that I still have a purpose for you. In fact, child, you have grown from the experience through which I have led you. You are now more sensitive to others, more resilient when minor problems arise. You know that I have led you through what seemed a most terrible time; now you realise that I will never leave you no matter what the future holds.

Beloved, I heal the broken-hearted. Rejoice, for I have healed you.

Ps. 147:3; Isa. 43:18–19.

45

He Died to Make You Whole

———— o ————

"Like one from whom men hide their faces he was despised, and we esteemed him not."

(Isa. 53:3)

I sent my Son to share in the frailty of your humanity. I sent him to suffer so that you could be set free from every bondage. I watched him suffer on the cross, refusing to intervene because this sacrifice was necessary to free you from your sin and every other negative affliction. It was necessary for my Son to suffer on behalf of the many who would become my sons in successive generations.

On the cross he was disfigured beyond recognition. The powers of darkness, and men in the grip of such powers, had done their worst. Now he was to emerge triumphant.

I want you to understand the full extent of what was happening when Jesus died for you. I want you to see how completely he identified with every situation of need in your life.

He had no beauty to attract people to him as he hung there. There was nothing in his appearance to make him desirable. And yet this was my Son!

Do you not see that he was identified completely with all who think of themselves as having no beauty; those who consider themselves unattractive either in appearance or personality? **He was one with the maimed and deformed**. He was dying to make them whole.

He has been despised not only by those who were responsible for the crucifixion, but also by men and women of successive generations who have despised him. Yes, **he died for those who despised him!** See how many despise him still. They blaspheme against him; they ridicule his teaching and ignore his claims. Still there are multitudes who serve other gods and so despise the One true God who gave his life for them. This is the measure of my love expressed in Jesus.

He tells you to love even your enemies because he has done that himself.

He suffered a life of rejection from those who opposed him. His ultimate rejection was more cruel than any rejection experienced by men. He was a man of sorrows and familiar with suffering. And he deserved nothing of this.

All who are despised can find their acceptance in him. All those who have been rejected can find their acceptance in him. All who have known sorrow find their consolation in the One who enters into their suffering with them. All who have experienced a life of suffering can find their answer in him.

Beloved, you are no longer despised or rejected by me. I don't afflict you with sorrow or suffering. You live in him, my beloved son, and he suffered that you may enjoy my acceptance and the life of my Spirit flowing through your life!

So is there a price you have to pay for your salvation? No! It has already been paid. Is there a cost for you to bear now that you are saved? Yes, it is to share in his suffering now!

Because you love him and live in him, some will despise you and reject you for your allegiance to him. What does this matter compared with the joy of knowing you are eternally accepted by me?

Like Jesus you will look around with sorrow for the lost; you will weep over the unsaved, those who spurn the salvation I offer through him.

Pray, beloved one, that my Kingdom will be extended; that others will put their faith in the atoning love of my Son, so that they may be brought out of darkness into his precious light.

Isa. 53:1–12; Col. 2:15; Matt. 5:44; 1 John 4:13; Rom. 8:17.

46

Signs and Wonders

———— o ————

"The seventy-two returned with joy and said, 'Lord, even the demons submit to us in your name.'"
(Luke 10:17)

H is disciples were awe-struck by the miracles and healings Jesus performed. It was usual to see crowds of people pressing forward wanting to be healed.

When their faith and expectancy had developed sufficiently, Jesus gave the disciples authority to heal. Some were diffident at first. It was one thing to watch Jesus; quite another to be sent out in his name to do similar things.

The works of power they performed were evidence of the truth they proclaimed concerning the Kingdom of God. As they preached the good news of the Kingdom they exercised their authority to heal and deliver people in the name of Jesus, and were delighted at the results. They were overjoyed that even the demons submitted to them in the power of his name.

Child, I give disciples the same authority today because it is the same gospel they proclaim. Those sent in my name are given the commission to proclaim the Kingdom of God in word and power. I want them to

believe that I will verify their message by signs and wonders attending their preaching.

They need not fear that I will fail them. So why don't more preachers today move in power and authority? Some are not truly commissioned by me, others don't believe I would use them in such ways. Others consider the message is enough in itself, without being prepared to prove it is the truth through demonstrations of my power. Sadly, when this is the case, they deprive my people of much blessing.

Jesus preached more effectively than anyone; but he confirmed the truth of his message with demonstrations of power! During the early years of the Church the apostles continued to believe that signs and wonders would accompany their preaching. Many still experience these things because I continue to give the same authority to my Church today. This power doesn't diminish in its effectiveness. Those who believe my word and exercise this authority see the results which bring great blessing to many people and authenticate the message they proclaim.

It saddens me, beloved, to hear some say they are content to preach the gospel without signs and wonders. I am pleased they want to preach the gospel; but in my mercy and love I want to meet the needs of my people. I want to save, heal and deliver. The more I do in the lives of my children, the more I am glorified in them. And every work of my grace blesses me. Thanksgiving ascends to my throne from grateful hearts.

Luke 10:16–20; Matt. 14:35–6; Mark 16:17–20; John 14:11–14; 1 Cor. 2:4–5.

47

Faith Produces Results

———— o ————

"But when he asks, he must believe and not doubt."
(Jas. 1:6)

Sometimes Jesus was disappointed with his disciples. He taught them the principles of faith, to use my supernatural resources and expect my intervention in response to their prayers.

When Jesus came down the mountain of transfiguration, nine disciples were trying to heal an epileptic boy. Apparently nothing had happened in response to their prayer. They were watching the boy writhe around on the ground, believing the symptoms rather than my victory over them.

What do people say in such situations? "They can't do it." "God doesn't want to heal him." "This kind is impossible to cure."

What did Jesus say? "O unbelieving and perverse generation, how long shall I stay with you? How long shall I put up with you? Bring the boy here to me."

He was indignant; **anything was possible for him, or for any who put their faith in him!**

After Jesus had healed the boy, the disciples asked him why they had not been successful. He didn't conceal the truth from them: **it was because of their little faith.** Such a condition could only be healed by praying with faith.

When Jesus addressed the demons causing the sickness, he had immediate victory and the healing was accomplished. **Faith always produces results and faith is expressed in authority.** Jesus received the result he expected.

This is true for you, beloved. **Faith is being sure about the outcome. It is being sure of what you hope for and certain of what you do not see.** There is no question mark with faith.

You wonder how you can have such certainty. Only by hearing my word, receiving it in your heart, believing what I say because it is I, your Lord, who has spoken.

Beloved, your faith is not in events, healings, deliverances. I am to be the object of your faith. **Your faith is in me and, therefore, in what I say.**

Heaven and earth will pass away; my words will never pass away. Hold fast to my words. Believe what I say about you, about your circumstances and concerning my purpose for you.

Jas. 1:5–8; Matt. 17:14–21; John 14:12; Heb. 11:1.

48

My Victory In You

———— ∘ ————

"But thanks be to God! He gives us the victory through our Lord Jesus Christ."

(1 Cor. 15:57)

Jesus did more than take your sin to the cross. He took you, the sinner. He not only took your sicknesses but the one who is sick. He not only took your need, but the one who has the need. He didn't die for sin, sickness and needs. He died for people, to deliver them from those afflictions. He died for you. He took every part of you so that you might belong to me totally and for ever.

You have been crucified with Christ. It is no longer you who live; it is he who lives in you. This became reality in your experience the day you put your faith in me. **The old person you were is dead and lies buried. I have raised you to a totally new life; you are a new creation.**

I placed you in Christ so that you can benefit from everything he has done. His life becomes your life. You live in him and he in you.

Enjoy the wonderful revelation of your inheritance. I have blessed you with every spiritual blessing in heavenly places; for all those blessings are in Christ, and you are in him. I promise to meet your every need according to my riches in glory. **You live in the glorious, victorious one.**

Do you realise that you live in his victory, that I always lead you in my triumphal procession in Christ? Many condemn themselves to a life of failure, fear and defeat because they think they have to win the victory. And whenever they fight they seem to lose. **It is difficult to win a victory that has already been won! True faith overcomes the world because it rests on the fact that Jesus has overcome, that he will not fail anyone who puts their trust in him.**

Let this revelation burn in your heart every day: you are in Christ and he is in you. His victory becomes your victory in every situation in which you place your trust in him. **Sin is defeated through Jesus. Sickness is defeated through Jesus. The devil is defeated through Jesus. Need is overcome through Jesus. I ALWAYS lead you in his triumphal procession.**

Beloved child, you will have problems and persecution; this is inevitable. If you realise the truth of what I am saying, you can be of good courage because Jesus has overcome the world. Believe my word and your circumstances will be changed. You don't need to live in failure and defeat any more.

Rom. 6:8; Gal. 2:20; 2 Cor. 2:14; 1 John 5:4; 1 John 4:4.

49

I Know You

—— o ——

"O Lord, you have searched me and you know me."
(Ps. 139:1)

I know all about you, child. I know when you sit down and when you rise. I perceive your thoughts from afar. Yes, you cannot hide even a thought from me.

I know when you believe the negative things which the devil and your own flesh suggest to you. I know when you worry and are anxious about your circumstances. I know when you take to heart the negative, accusing things others say to you, instead of protecting yourself with the shield of faith.

I know when you go out and when you lie down. I am familiar with all your ways. Before a word is on your tongue I know it completely. Yes, I know your heart, child.

I know you can't suddenly change your thought patterns and your heart when you pray.

Many pray what seem to be prayers of faith and are then perplexed as to why they apparently aren't answered. I alone know when someone believes. I know when there is genuine faith in the heart, for it is sustained between the times of prayer.

Have you not noticed that some needs have been met even before you have prayed about them? This is because I have seen the faith in your heart. At such times I don't have to wait for your prayer times to answer you!

You have sometimes wondered about my command to pray continually, haven't you? This seems unrealistic to you and you have considered it only possible for someone far more spiritual than you!

But you see, beloved, if I know all your thoughts there is a sense in which you do pray continually. Can you now see the importance of rejecting immediately every negative thought that denies faith in my word? You need to take every thought and make it obedient to Christ.

Remember, it only takes a little yeast of negativity to work through the whole lump. So I say these things to you for your own good.

You see, beloved, I surround you in my love because I want the best for you. I hem you in behind and before.

Are these thoughts too wonderful for you? There is nowhere you can go to escape my presence. I will not take my Spirit from you, even when I see criticism, negativity and unbelief in your heart.

My hand is upon you. I have called you and chosen you for myself. I have created your innermost being to house my presence. You are fearfully and wonderfully made, beloved child!

Beloved, I have made you for faith, not unbelief; for love, not selfishness; for joy, not heaviness; for peace,

not anxiety; for fulfilment, not frustration. Abide in me.

Ps. 139:1–4; 1 Thess. 5:17; 2 Cor. 10:5; John 15:4.

50

I Am Changing You

———— o ————

"Be transformed by the renewing of your mind. Then
you will be able to test and approve what God's will
is – his good, pleasing and perfect will."

(Rom. 12:2)

Beloved, you look at yourself and see so much that
is still not like Jesus, ways in which you fail to reflect
the life and righteousness of my Son.

As it was my purpose to place you in Jesus, so it is
my plan to change you into his likeness.

When Jesus took Peter, James and John up the mountain of transfiguration, his appearance was suddenly
changed. Until then they had seen him in his humanity;
suddenly they were confronted with him in his glory.

Because of his perfection, this transformation could
take place in a moment of time. With you it is different.
Because of your imperfection I have to change you by
stages, from one degree of glory to another. My Spirit
lives within you to effect these changes.

How will the transformation take place? By the
renewing of your thinking. This is my word: **You are to
be transfigured by the renewing of your mind. I want
to change your thinking to bring it into line with my**

thinking. The more you think like me, the more like me you become.

So I want you to understand my word. I want it to be revelation to you. Your thinking needs to change whenever you disagree with my word.

Far from restricting your intellect, my word will challenge the limited confines of your thinking. My Spirit will encourage you to think supernaturally. He will expand your thinking, not stifle it.

The proud set their intellects above my word and are guilty of unbelief. **The humble realise that my thoughts are higher than their thoughts!**

Beloved, have faith in my word. Let your mind be renewed, your natural thought patterns changed so that you know my good, acceptable and perfect will.

2 Cor. 3:18; Matt. 17:1–8; Col. 3:2.

51

A New Creation

——— ○ ———

"For you died, and your life is now hidden with Christ in God." (Col. 3:3)

You are blessed because you live in the One who gives blessing, and he lives in you!

You are righteous because you live in the One who is righteous and he lives in you! He has cleansed you from all your unrighteousness.

You are holy because you live in the Holy One, and the Holy One lives in you.

You are filled with love because you live in the One who is love, and the One who is love lives in you.

You live in the Mighty One and his power is in you.

You live in the One who is joy and he lives in you.

You live in the Prince of Peace and he lives in you.

You live in the Merciful One and he lives in you.

Are you getting the idea, beloved? It is not who you once were that matters, but who you are now! See yourself as the new creation that you are. That is why Jesus said: Abide in me and I in you.

Col. 3:1–3; 1 Cor. 1:30; John 15:4.

52

The Bread of Life

———— o ————

**"I am the bread of life. He who comes to me will never
go hungry."**

(John 6:35)

Beloved child, I have given you the true bread from
heaven: Jesus! Feed on him daily by feeding on his
words of truth and life. He taught you to pray: "Give
us today our daily bread." Do you think that refers only
to physical food? I want to nourish you spiritually as
well as physically. Work for the food that endures to
eternal life, the food Jesus gives you.

Everyone who listens to my voice comes to Jesus and
receives eternal life through him. He is the way of salvation that I have provided.

What does it mean to feed on the words of Jesus?
Listen to what he says. Believe him. Put what he says
into operation. Receive the life that is in his words.

**"To all who received him, to those who believed
in his name, he gave the right to become children of
God."**

**"From the fullness of his grace we have all received
one blessing after another."**

"Whoever believes in him is not condemned."

"Whoever believes in the Son has eternal life."

"The work of God is this: to believe in the one he has sent."

"The one who feeds on me will live because of me."

"He who feeds on this bread will live for ever."

Child, I have set a feast before you; you need never go hungry. And these few scriptures are only a tiny part of the feast!

John 6:32–40; John 1:12; John 3:16–18; John 3:36; John 6:29; John 6:57; John 6:58.

53

Jesus Is Truth

———— ∘ ————

"For this I came into the world, to testify to the truth. Everyone on the side of truth listens to me."

(John 18:37)

Jesus is the truth. To disagree with what he says is to disagree with me. **You cannot separate Jesus from the words I gave him to speak. To deny what he says is to deny the way in which I have chosen to reveal myself.** To disobey his words is to choose another path.

The entrance of my words into your heart brings light. When people believe that which contradicts my word they embrace darkness. Don't exalt your reason above the revelation I have given of myself through Jesus. Walk in my truth, as if your hand is held out to me to lead and guide you.

You are learning that there are four main things which fight against faith in what I say. **First there is your reason. This is to be the servant of my word, not its judge.** For my word will expand your thinking, but your reason will diminish the effectiveness of my truth in your life. I have given you the ability to reason **so that you can understand the revelation of my word;** your reason will also show you how to apply it so that what I say is translated into action.

Secondly, circumstances often contradict my word. You are learning that as you believe what I say, faith changes the circumstances. I will not reduce my word to the level of your experience. **My purpose is to raise the level of your experience to my word.**

Thirdly, your feelings disagree with my word on many occasions. This is because your feelings are often influenced by your circumstances. Notice how easily feelings change, whereas my word will never change. So which is more reliable? When you believe what I say, my word will influence your emotions. **There is no greater feeling than having complete confidence in my word; no greater joy than that which accompanies faith.**

Fourthly, the enemy tries to undermine your confidence in my word. You need to take up the shield of faith with which you are able to quench all his fiery darts, all his lying accusations and insinuations.

You are learning, beloved, that you need to know my word, study my word, receive my word, believe my word and live in the good of my word. And you have my promise: "If you live in me and my words live in you, ask whatever you wish, and it will be given you."

John 18:37; Jas. 1:22; John 8:31–2; Eph. 6:16.

54

The Disciples Leave Jesus

———— o ————

"We know that we have come to know him if we obey his commands . . . Whoever claims to live in him must walk as Jesus did."

(1 John 2:3,6)

Many of his disciples turned back and no longer followed Jesus when they couldn't accept all that he said. He didn't run after them or try to persuade them to remain. He didn't offer to compromise his words or the style of his ministry to accommodate them. He watched them leave. Many of them!

Then he asked the Twelve if they too wanted to leave him. Do you understand what was happening here?

Jesus would never impose his will on anyone. He would never force anyone to believe his words or obey the truth. The response of every individual must be freely given in love.

Many want to create a religion of their own, choosing to believe what appeals to them and leaving the rest. This does not fool me! True disciples understand that a Christian is one who believes in Jesus and therefore accepts **all** that he says. There is no room for disagreement with what I say through my Son. It is for each individual either to accept or reject what he says. If they reject his words, they reject him. And if they reject him they reject me.

I **always** lead you in triumphal procession in Christ. This is only possible because you believe what I say. Some don't like such talk. They dismiss it as triumphalism. But it is the revelation of my word. It is my purpose to lead you in triumph – **always**. You wouldn't expect me to lead you in failure, would you, child?

Those who don't like triumphal talk clearly do not live in victory. They don't believe what I say, which is why they are not more triumphant.

Because you believe me, you can expect me to lead you through any situation victoriously, no matter how difficult it may appear. Don't be like those who turned away. Rather be as one who follows. I will lead you through every time of fear, failure, difficulty and opposition to my victory!

Jesus was able to discern what was in the hearts of those who turned away from him. He knew that without true love for him they would neither believe nor obey his word.

This is not true of you, child, is it? You love Jesus. You want to believe and obey his word, don't you? I know you fail sometimes; but I am merciful. I never cast away those who come to me. If some choose to turn away that is their decision; I give them the freedom to do so. If they choose to disbelieve my words they cannot reap the rewards of faith. If they choose to disobey my words they miss the rewards which come from obedience.

Beloved, I want you to reap the rewards of faith and

obedience. You are a believer. I call you to be a faithful disciple, but will never force you to conform to my ways. I will lead; you follow!

1 John 2:3–6; John 6:60–8; Luke 10:16; 2 Cor. 2:14.

55

The Authority of My Word

———— ∘ ————

**"Do not merely listen to the word, and so deceive your-
selves. Do what it says."**

(Jas. 1:22)

Never had people heard anyone speak with such
authority. Yet not all wanted to submit to him. The
religious leaders were challenged by his words. They
had only the authority of their ecclesiastical positions;
Jesus demonstrated authority from heaven. They were
no match for this; so they resolved to destroy him.

They were jealous of his miracles and healings. They
were content with a religion of outward observances,
rather than true holiness or submission to my will. They
were more interested in law than love. They wanted
worldly prestige more than supernatural power to meet
the needs of my people.

Even though his religious enemies didn't recognise
Jesus, demons did. When he spoke they cried out,
unable to conceal their presence. They knew him to be
the Holy One of God. He silenced them, refusing
to allow them to speak. He commanded them to
leave those they had bound. He demonstrated that the
power and authority of my Kingdom is greater than
any man-made religious activity, or any evil power or
spirit.

Dear child, you recognise my authority in Jesus. You honour me as your Lord. You are discovering that I am not interested in a religion of external appearances or traditions. The authority of my word is to take precedence over any of your traditions. **To acknowledge my authority is to acknowledge the authority of my word in your life.**

So don't be like the Pharisees who rejected what Jesus said. Bring every aspect of your life into line with my word. Ensure that your thinking agrees with what I say; that your speech in no way contradicts my truth, and that your actions reflect what Jesus would do in your situation.

The more you submit to my authority in this way, beloved, the more you will be able to speak and act with authority. Those who live by faith in Jesus are people of authority.

Jas. 1:19–25; Matt. 7:28; Matt. 12:9–14; Matt. 9:28–32; John 14:12–14.

56

Who Do You Say I Am?

—— ○ ——

"Simon Peter answered, 'You are the Christ, the Son of the living God.'"

(Matt. 16:16)

It was a simple question: "Who do you say I am?" The faith of Jesus' disciples hung on their answer. Peter boldly proclaimed him to be the Christ, the Messiah, my Anointed One, my Son.

Can you imagine his joy and relief when Jesus congratulated him on the answer? These men had been wondering, hardly daring to believe it could be true, afraid to make any such public statement – until this moment! You can imagine Peter's relief and the awe those men felt!

Simon Peter was blessed by receiving such a heaven-sent revelation, and through having the boldness to declare it. Jesus called him Peter, meaning "boulder". Jesus would build his Church, not on a boulder, but on himself, the immeasurable bedrock. That boulder was resting on the bedrock of Jesus. Hell could not prevail against the Church built on the foundation of Jesus himself.

Then Jesus said to Peter: "I give you the keys to the Kingdom of heaven." The keys were the symbol of authority. Because he recognised Jesus to be my Son and had put his faith in him, he was being given the authority of the Kingdom which far outweighs the enemy's power.

You recognise Jesus to be the Christ; you believe him to be my Son, don't you, child? Very well, then, **I give you the keys, the authority of my Kingdom,** so that you too may play your part in the building of my Church.

You have authority over all the power of the evil one; nothing will harm you as you exercise that authority over whatever opposes you. You have the power to bind and loose. You have the authority to forgive or to refuse to forgive.

You have the power and authority to pray and act in the name of Jesus. I want you to understand the great power that is available to you as a believer.

However, I don't want you to make the mistake Peter made. Now they knew him to be the Messiah, Jesus chose this moment to tell his disciples that he would be rejected and killed, but raised to life on the third day.

This didn't fit in at all with Peter's preconceived ideas of Messiahship. So he took Jesus aside and rebuked him for suggesting such a thing!

Jesus said to Peter: "Get behind me, Satan! You are a stumbling-block to me; you do not have in mind the things of God, but the things of men."

Can you sense the sting in these remarks? Can you imagine how Peter felt? One moment being congratulated because he was voicing revelation from heaven; yet soon afterwards being told he was a mouthpiece of Satan!

Yes, these remarks stung Peter to the heart; and they were meant to. Jesus had to teach him a very important lesson. If he recognised him to be my Son, it was not his place to rebuke Jesus, to disagree or argue with him. He needed to believe all that Jesus told him.

Peter was thinking in natural terms, no longer with revelation. When he rebuked Jesus he didn't have in mind the things of God.

Beloved child, I want you to believe everything that Jesus says. I want you to have his words in mind and not to argue with him, even when you find it difficult to understand or agree with what he says. He is the truth!

Of course, what Jesus said was fulfilled, and it is because of those events that you have become my child. All his words shall surely come to pass!

Matt. 16:13–19; Matt. 16:21–3; Matt. 24:35.

57

Binding and Loosing

———— o ————

"Whatever you bind on earth will be bound in heaven, and whatever you loose on earth will be loosed in heaven."

(Matt. 16:19)

Beloved, whatever Jesus says you can do, you can do! Don't argue or disagree with him.

You have the authority of one who belongs to my Kingdom. Whatever you bind on earth will be bound in heaven. This means that whatever you prevent on earth is prevented in heaven. Do you understand? **You have authority to prevent on earth what I do not allow in heaven.** Exercise that authority in the name of Jesus.

Whatever you loose on earth is loosed in heaven. **You can permit and enable whatever heaven permits.**

You have the authority to prevent what Jesus prevented, and to permit what he permitted. If you do this, you will truly fulfil my word that everything you do is to be done in the name of the Lord Jesus, giving thanks to me through him. Heaven stands behind your proper use of the authority I have given you.

This is the kind of authority I want my Church to exercise so that it will influence the society in which it is set. The trouble is that many of my children act with diffidence rather than with true authority. They don't appreciate what great power they can exercise, especially when they agree together in faith.

Jesus promised that I will do whatever is agreed in faith by **any** two of my children. Don't repeat Peter's mistake and rebuke Jesus. Submit yourself to what he says; don't argue with him!

Does this conflict with your experience? I alone can see what is in the hearts of my children; I know when any two truly agree.

And notice, child, this is a word about **ANY** two agreeing. So it is addressed to you!

If two agree in faith they both exercise their authority to prevent what is opposed to my heavenly will. They are prepared to address the situation with authority, speaking to the mountain and commanding it to be moved. They both agree to loose my power or provision into the situation. When they do these things it is in the sure and certain knowledge that what they say shall surely come to pass. There is no doubt in their minds as to the outcome, so sure is their trust in my word and my faithfulness.

These two are not alone in their agreeing, for when they come together in his name, Jesus is with them as he has promised. He gives them every encouragement to agree together, to speak with authority and pray with faith.

Beloved, faith is bold. Do you remember what I told Joshua? He was to be bold and very courageous. And if he was careful to obey all that was written in my word,

I promised he would be prosperous and successful! He would inherit the land!

Matt. 16:13–19; Matt. 18:19; Jas. 1:6; Josh. 1:7.

58

Your Victory Over The Enemy

———— o ————

"I have given you authority . . . to overcome all the power of the enemy."

(Luke 10:19)

The enemy is a deceiver. He is the thief who kills, steals and destroys. He brings conflict, confusion and violence into peoples' lives. Yet I have given you authority over all the powers of the evil one.

Once you were part of his domain. But when you put your faith in Jesus, I transferred you from his dominion and placed you in the Kingdom of my Son. **This means that the devil now has no hold over you, neither does he have any claim to your life.**

I rejoice every time I see someone delivered and set free from his clutches. This is one of the reasons I cause heaven to rejoice over every sinner who repents. Those who have been set free through their faith in Jesus, are to exercise their authority over the evil one. If they resist him, he will flee from them.

Don't be deceived by his devices. Don't allow him to condemn you falsely. Don't listen to the negative thoughts he wants to plant in your mind. He suggests that I don't truly love you, that I don't accept you or want you as my child. He reminds you of your failures, tries to rob you of your confidence and encourages you to look back at your past.

So don't speak as if you believe he has some kind of hold over you, that he has you bound in any way or the right to oppress you.

Live in the freedom I have given you in Jesus. You are a child of the King of heaven. You share my reign because you are part of my Kingdom. Jesus is to rule over you, not Satan. You share Jesus' victory and authority over every demonic force. You are able to say "No" to every temptation the enemy places before you.

You have the power to overcome him in every situation in your life because Jesus has disarmed the powers and authorities. He made a public spectacle of them, triumphing over them by the cross.

Beloved, you live in the good of his victory!

Luke 10:18–20; John 8:36; Jas. 4:7; Col. 2:13–15.

59

Your Authority Over The Enemy

——— o ———

"Resist the devil, and he will flee from you."

(Jas. 4:7)

Dear child, no doubt you are aware that many people today don't believe in the existence of demons. They use psychological jargon to describe the problems of the possessed; but can do nothing to set them free. This unwillingness to believe in demons is consistent with their unbelief in a personal devil.

I want you to be informed about the devil, not to be afraid of him. I want you to understand the tactics of the one who opposes you.

In my word he is described in a variety of ways. He is a real person; Jesus confronted him as such. He is the adversary who opposes me and those who belong to me. He is the god of this world who seeks to set up his own world-order in opposition to my Kingdom. He is the deceiver, even of the brethren, my children. He accuses them to try and bring them into condemnation.

He is the enemy who tempts people to sin. He is the father of lies, a liar from the beginning, the wicked one.

He is the prince of this world. He is an angel with a body, soul and spirit like all other angels. His kingdom is divided into principalities and powers in heavenly places. He rules over all the fallen angels, demons of various kinds and fallen mankind.

Yet the One who lives in you is greater than he! So you don't have to fear him. His kingdom cannot prevail against mine. He is already a defeated foe.

Once an archangel in heaven, Jesus witnessed his fall as soon as he rebelled against me. That fall was as swift as a flash of lightning. He has been given leave to roam to and fro over the face of the earth. His attacks on my children serve to test their hearts, to see if they will trust in me. But never lose sight of the fact that he is a thief who wants to steal, kill and destroy.

If you allow him, he will steal your joy, peace and health. He will try to undermine your trust in my word and faith in my love. But he cannot snatch you from my hand. **You have the shield of faith with which to put out all the fiery arrows he throws at you. If you resist him he will flee from you.**

You see, child, you possess an authority greater than his. You have heaven backing you. But you still need to be on the watch. The devil prowls around like an angry, mortally-wounded lion, looking for someone to devour.

Jesus delivered that mortal wound on the cross. There is nothing the enemy can do to avoid the fate which awaits him. **He is afraid of you when you use your Kingdom authority because you can inflict on him one defeat after another.**

1 John 4:4; John 8:44; Eph. 6:10–17; 1 Pet. 5:8–9.

60

Your Authority Over Demons

———— ◦ ————

"In my name they will drive out demons."
(Mark 16:17)

Demons are as real as the devil himself. They are disembodied spirits who seek a body within which to live and through which to work.

There were several occasions when Jesus confronted these evil spirits within people. They could recognise him as the Holy One of God, even before people knew he had come from heaven and had power over them.

Jesus silenced them. The revelation concerning his identity would come at the right time and in the right way; certainly not through demons!

Notice that Jesus didn't fight these demons; he commanded them. His authority was greater than the one who ruled them.

There is no point in you talking with deceiving spirits, child. When you are confronted with demons, follow Jesus' example and command them to leave in his name. **If you expect a battle, you will have a battle; if you expect victory, you will have victory.**

You have that victory in Jesus. In every confrontation you are proclaiming the victory he has already won.

This is what it means to use the name and authority of Jesus.

I am not sending you out to look for demons. I am telling you to overcome them whenever you come across them.

The enemy will try to explain these things away. People who are deceived by him will suggest that Jesus only referred to demons because he used the thought-forms of his day. This is blasphemous talk. Jesus was neither deceived, nor did he deceive others. He would not have spoken to powers that did not exist, or refer to demons if they were only the figment of people's imaginations. He corrected their thinking about many other matters. If they were wrong about having a belief in demons, Jesus would have corrected their error immediately. He certainly would not have spoken to spiritual forces that didn't exist!

Consider the results when he confronted these spiritual powers. People were immediately set free from their control and influence. Jesus didn't take anyone through a process of psycho-analysis; he simply set them free! And it was not unusual for this to be done with violent manifestations.

Most dramatic was his deliverance of the man called Legion, because so many demons lived in him. Jesus didn't command them to leave one by one. They were all commanded to leave at once. Jesus allowed them to inhabit the pigs who immediately ran into the lake and drowned.

This shows the destructive nature of Satan's work, but also that there is no equal conflict between good and evil. **The power and authority of my Kingdom is**

vastly superior to that of the enemy. Whenever light comes against darkness, the light prevails. The darkness cannot overcome Jesus, or those who put their trust in him.

Mark 16:15–18; Luke 4:35; John 8:12.

61

My Anointing Gives You Authority

———— o ————

"But you will receive power when the Holy Spirit comes on you."

(Acts 1:8)

Beloved child, because you have received my Spirit, like Jesus you have the anointing of the Holy One. My anointing lives in you. Yes, the same divine Spirit who lived in Jesus lives in you!

I want you to live in the full potential of what I have made possible for you. You have both the power and authority to live as Jesus did. He said that anyone who believes in him could do the same things and greater things still because he was returning to me in heaven, when he asked me to pour out my Spirit on all who believed in him.

Beloved, you are a believer! Don't waste what I have given you. **You can do the same things and greater things still;** that is his promise. You have authority to pray and act in the name of Jesus. Don't listen to the voice of unbelief. Believe what I say!

Believe that I have given you what my word says I have given you. Do what I say you are able to do. The power of my Spirit within you enables you to do whatever I ask of you. Use the faith and authority I have given you and you will not fail me.

You have authority to do whatever I tell you to do in my word. That authority is greater than any worldly or ecclesiastical authority.

You have authority over all the power of the evil one. Your authority is greater than any demonic power that opposes you.

You have authority to pray in the name of Jesus, expecting to receive the answer you need.

Exercise this authority today in the reactions you have to circumstances which arise; in the way you stand against the accusing tactics of the enemy, in the way you speak to others and the confidence with which you pray. Begin with small matters if you are not used to exercising such authority and your faith will enlarge. You will soon realise that you can address much bigger issues with a confidence and determination that was lacking previously.

The anointing of the Holy One gives you authority to heal the sick, to cast out demons; you can even raise the dead! You will only use such authority effectively if, like Jesus, you faithfully obey the leading of my Holy Spirit. He gives you the power and authority to do what he leads you to do, not what you want to do for your own selfish reasons.

I ask nothing more of you than that you listen to my Spirit of truth and do what he says. You will be amazed at the results!

1 John 2:20; John 12:49; John 14:12–14; John 16:13–15.

62

My Name Is Exalted

———— o ————

"For you have exalted above all things your name and your word."

(Ps. 138:2)

M y dear son, I exalt my name and my word above all things. I want you to see what this means for you.

You know my name is higher than any other name; my authority is therefore greater than any other authority. I tell you to do everything in my name; that means with my authority. If there is something you want to do, but cannot do it with my authority, this is a sure indication that I don't want you to do it. You are in danger of exalting that thing, whatever it is, above my name. You will never prosper by doing that. Everything in your life is to be under my authority.

I exalt my name above **all** things. Don't compromise about this. **Above all things.** Acknowledge my Lordship and Sovereignty in **every** area of your life. I tell you this for your own good.

Because I love you, beloved, I want the very best for you. You cannot enjoy my best while contending against my authority.

Why do I tell you to rejoice in me always? Because this demonstrates that you are exalting my name above your

circumstances and feelings. When you do that it is possible for me to intervene and change those circumstances.

Do I not say that you are to give thanks in all circumstances? Why? Because then you are exalting my name above your own natural thinking. You realise that I am greater than the situation, that I am with you in the middle of the mess, muddle and confusion which sometimes seems to beset you. Your trust is in me, not in the circumstances. And I rejoice in this.

You see, beloved, if I exalt my name above all things, I exalt it above any problem or situation that could arise in your life. If this is what I do, it is what you are to do. Then my reign can be brought into effect in these particular circumstances.

At last you are beginning to realise that I want the best for you. This is why I tell you to speak to the mountains of need and command them to move. I wouldn't tell you to move things I had caused or wanted in your life.

Your ability to speak effectively to the mountains depends on your authority. And that authority is dependent on faith. **And that faith is the product of believing that my name is greater than any situation and is therefore to be exalted above all things.**

It is not until you rejoice in me and give thanks that your faith starts to operate. And I always respond to faith.

Until that moment you have exalted your doubt, fear and unbelief above my name. As soon as you exalt my name above all things, things begin to happen!

Phil. 4:4; 1 Thess. 5:18; Matt. 17:20.

63

My Word Is Exalted

——— o ———

"I will walk about in freedom, for I have sought out your precepts."

(Ps. 119:45)

I also exalt my word above everything. Therefore you are to do the same. **If you exalt my name above all things, you will inevitably exalt my word above everything. Likewise, the one who exalts my word above all things, exalts my name also.** These two are indivisible.

What does it mean to exalt my word above everything?

You have grown up with natural thought patterns, many of which have been negative. You have been taught to exalt your reasoning powers.

Some of my children imagine they have discovered new techniques of counselling and ministry that are an improvement on my word. They claim a better perception into the way people function than Jesus had! They do things so differently from him, taking people back into their pasts looking for ways to liberate them. Would you go to your dustbin if you wanted to prepare a good meal? Would you not go to the store cupboard and use fresh food? The remnants of past meals are rightly discarded for ever.

People will only be free to live in the good of the new life I have given them by coming to the store house of my word and feeding on my truth. **Going back to the old life can never give faith to live the new life.**

If you exalt my word above all things, you exalt my word above your past, above your feelings, above your doubts, above your hurts and sense of inadequacy; above your rejection and failure, above your symptoms and sickness. And what is the outcome when you do this?

Your past is dead, buried and finished with; you have been made new. Why dig up the corpse? That is what the enemy wants you to do; anything to tempt you to doubt that it is for freedom that Christ has already set you free!

Your feelings are not the truth when they conflict with my word. When you listen to your doubts and fears you have stopped listening to me!

My words are healing for your hurts, for every sickness of spirit, soul or body. You are no longer rejected but accepted in my beloved Son.

Beloved, don't dig up the past; the rotten with all its stinking corruption. Believe what I have done for you. **Exalt my word above your past and present circumstances.** Only in this way can you live the life of faith to which I call you. That is a life of freedom.

Those who believe that the past is the truth about them, live trapped in their past. **But those who believe what my Son has done on the cross are liberated from their past!**

Ps. 138:2; 2 Cor. 5:17; Rom. 6:3–4.

64

What Love!

———— o ————

"He who loves me will be loved by my Father, and I too will love him and show myself to him."
(John 14:21)

It was an act of utter devotion. She used very expensive ointment. She anointed Jesus' feet and wiped them with her long, dark hair. What love!

Judas was outraged: "What a waste," he said. The money could have been given to the poor.

Mary lavished her love on Jesus without thought of the cost. **Only true love could inspire such generosity.**

Nothing is wasted when given in worship. Judas missed the whole point of what was happening; he didn't have such love for me.

Mary will always be remembered because of her act of love; and Judas for his betrayal of love. I rejoice, beloved, that you love me. So don't consider anything too valuable to give to me! Love me with all of your heart, soul, mind and strength. And know that you can only love me because I have first loved you.

John 12:1–8; Phil. 3:7–9.

65

My Love

"As the Father has loved me, so have I loved you. Now remain in my love."

(John 15:9)

I loved Jesus perfectly. He knew I would never fail him, never leave him. He could always trust in my faithfulness.

When he commanded sickness to leave; I healed. When he called Lazarus from the tomb; I raised him. When he addressed the storm; I calmed the waves and the wind. When he lay in the coldness of the tomb; I raised him.

He could do nothing himself; he knew how important it was to listen to me, therefore. Because he lived in dependence on me I gave him the words to speak and showed him what to do.

He could face the cross, knowing he would have to experience separation from me as part of the cost because he could trust in my unfailing love, a perfect love that would never fail him.

Now, beloved child, in the same way that I love Jesus, so he loves you. You can depend on him for he will never leave you nor forsake you. He will be with you always. It is important for you to listen to the voice of his Spirit and let him show you what to do.

Just as he could do nothing of himself, so it is true that apart from him you can do nothing. **He will give you the words to speak and will show you what to do.** When you speak with faith to mountains of need, he will move them. When you command sickness to leave in his name, he will remove it. You are able to do the same things as Jesus if you are secure in his love.

Don't think of yourself as being isolated or alone. I am watching over you, beloved child, concerned for your welfare, rejoicing in the song of love for me that fills your heart. **I am holding you in my perfect love every day of your life.**

Even when you feel battered and bruised by events, I am there with you, ready to talk, encourage and heal your wounds.

This perfect love doesn't change with circumstances; it is constant day by day. Know, beloved, that there is never a moment of time when I fail to love you with my perfect love.

John 11:43; John 12:49; John 15:1–17; John 14:12–14.

66

Love God

———— o ————

"Love the Lord your God with all your heart and with all your soul and with all your strength."

(Deut. 6:5)

My dear child, I love you with an everlasting love, a perfect love. Love desires a response of love, or it is frustrated. Consider how my love for so many is frustrated by their indifference to me and even hatred. Yet I continue to love them because it is my nature to love.

You see this love in Jesus as he prayed for those responsible for his crucifixion. Even as they nailed him to the cross he asked me to forgive them because they acted in ignorance.

I have revealed my love to you, child, and have given you many evidences of that love, haven't I? Do you not understand that I long for a whole-hearted response of love from you?

The law embodied the command to love me with all your heart, mind, soul and strength. I am well aware that the law states what I require, but is powerless to enable my will. However, you have received my Spirit, and he is love! You have the resources within you to love me as I desire.

Do you want to love me with all your heart? Or do you treasure other people and things above me?

Do you want to love me with all your mind? Or do you still value your own reason, opinions and thoughts above the authority of my word?

Do you want to love me with all your soul? Are you prepared to submit your will to mine so that in love you are ready to obey me? Is this what you want?

Do you want to love me with all your strength? Or are there other things distracting you, sapping your energy and causing you to be less effective in the work of my Kingdom?

I cannot force you to love; it has to be your own choice to respond to my love for you.

Actions speak louder than words. You can answer these questions in the affirmative and still not do these things. You may be sincere in your answers, **but obedience demands more of you than sincerity.** Your will is involved, not only as you answer the questions, but as you live out these answers day by day.

Jer. 31:3; Luke 23:32–4; Jas. 1:22.

67

Love Is Patient And Kind

—— ∘ ——

"Love is patient, love is kind."

(1 Cor. 13:4)

My child, I am not demanding. See how patient I have been with you, waiting for your love for me to rise up like a flame in your heart. I have seen you through times when your love had grown cold; you had drifted back to your own ways instead of walking in mine.

I have forgiven you and watched my love being rekindled in your heart. You have fallen in love with me all over again! Your desire for prayer is restored, your excitement with my word returns, and you long to be of service to me. Then the flesh makes its demands on you and all too often you have compromised your love for me, haven't you?

There have been times when you have justified your actions, claiming they are consistent with my love. Yet your need to justify what you have done points to the fact that you are far from convinced yourself about the rightness of your actions.

Again I have waited patiently as you work through these internal conflicts and come back to a whole-hearted submission to my will.

You see, child, however you treat me does not affect my love for you. My love is expressed in kindness as well as patience. **I want to see in you the same consistency of love for me as I have for you; a love that is manifested in practical obedience to my word and the leading of my Holy Spirit. A love that is patient with others as I am with you. A love that is kind and generous towards others because this is how I treat you.**

See how gentle I am with you! The greatest times of fulfilment in your life are when you live in loving obedience to me, when you love others as I love you. At such times you have a sense of peace and well-being, knowing you are one with me and have pleased me. And that is more precious than anything else, isn't it?

So don't allow other things to intrude, destroying your peace and causing you to compromise your love for me. That is good advice, isn't it, child?

1 Cor. 13:1–13; Rom. 7:22; 1 John 3:11–24.

68

The Nature of My Love

———— ○ ————

"It does not envy, it does not boast, it is not proud."
(1 Cor. 13:4)

Beloved child, if you realise the wonder of my love for you and the full extent of the inheritance I have given you, there will be no cause for you to envy anyone else.

I love you. Because I can do nothing imperfectly, I love you with a perfect love, in the same way that I loved Jesus. There can be no one in heaven or on earth whom I love more than you.

This is the truth, which has nothing to do with feelings. Sometimes you think I must love others more because you see the ways in which I bless them, answer their prayers, heal and anoint them for service. You admire their boldness of faith and their air of confidence. You wonder that others should apparently enjoy such a wonderful relationship with me and find it so easy to hear my voice.

Listen, child, I don't love them any more than I love you. It is true that some believe and trust in my love more than you; this is why I am able to use them in the way I do. However, they don't hinder you in your faith.

You would fare much better by looking to me rather than concentrating on others and being envious of them. The more you trust in my love, the more the qualities you admire in others shall be expressed in your own life.

And I want you to be pleased about the way you see my life expressed in others. Be thankful for their love and faithfulness. Let them be an example to you.

Also you are to heed this warning: what my Spirit does in others does not give them any right to boast. If they become proud I stop using them in the same ways. **It is only those who continue to be humble, giving me all the glory, that I will use in greater ways.**

Remember what Jesus said: **"Everyone who exalts himself will be humbled, and he who humbles himself will be exalted."**

Beloved, you will find that those I use effectively are not those who claim the highest place for themselves. They would prefer a lower place, but I have raised them up because of their simple trust in my love. They don't seek glory for themselves; they want to add glory to my name.

1 Cor. 13:1–13; 1 Pet. 5:5; Luke 14:11.

69

You Are Improving!

———— o ————

"It is not rude, it is not self-seeking, it is not easily angered."

(1 Cor. 13:5)

There are some things, beloved, that conceal rather than reveal my love. Rudeness is one of them. My love is gentle, gracious and strong. In Jesus it was expressed together with great authority, yet never rudeness.

He spoke at times with obvious anger and disappointment. But his anger was not an unrighteous response to events; he was expressing my righteous indignation.

He warned the Pharisees and other religious leaders that they were in danger of cursing themselves because of their opposition to him and the way they tried to prevent others receiving the gift of my Kingdom. He cleansed the Temple precincts of the traders and money-changers with the words: "It is written; my house will be called a house of prayer, but you are making it a 'den of robbers'."

These were actions prompted by love: love for my people to whom the gospel was being given, love for me and the place I had set aside for my presence amongst my people.

Jesus was not easily angered; but he did express my righteous wrath when necessary. He was angry with sin, because sin makes me angry. You can be thankful, beloved, that my anger lasts only for a moment, my favour for a lifetime!

To the disciples Jesus said: "O unbelieving and perverse generation! How much longer must I be with you?" When Peter allowed himself to be a mouthpiece for the enemy, he said: "Get behind me, Satan, you are on the side of the enemy, not of God."

All these were words coming from a heart of love. He was concerned that the disciples always acted with faith, that Peter should never disagree with his words.

The question you need to ask yourself, beloved, is this: **when you are angry, is this a sinful reaction to events or do you have the honour of my name at heart?** Is there a good, righteous cause for your anger?

When others are rude to you, don't retaliate in kind. Be loving and gracious. Don't allow your reactions to be prompted by selfish motives. Sometimes you are angry because you can't have your own way, or your plans have been interrupted. You have even been angry with me because the requirements of my love have impinged on your own selfish desires!

Be encouraged, beloved. See how different you are now compared with the way you used to react before you knew me. My Spirit has certainly been working within you, hasn't he? There is not so much rudeness, self-seeking or anger as there used to be, is there? You see, you are making progress. Good!

1 Cor. 13:1–13; Jas. 1:19–20; Eph. 4:26; Phil. 2:3; Matt. 17:14–21.

70

Love Keeps No Record of Wrongs

———— o ————

"Above all, love each other deeply, because love covers over a multitude of sins."

(1 Pet. 4:8)

My dear child, **love keeps no record of wrongs.** When I forgive you I forget the offence. I don't store up a list of your sins in my memory for future judgment. You will never be judged for the sins I have forgiven. When I forgive, I forget.

You have received mercy from me again and again. Therefore I want you to be merciful, to forgive even as I forgive you.

You don't keep any record of wrongs of those you love. You are happy to forget the offence that has momentarily disturbed your relationship. And you are relieved when those who love you extend such forgiveness to you. You have discovered that such mutual forgiveness makes the relationship sweet.

However, there are other occasions when you struggle with this whole business of forgiveness. You know you ought to forgive but find it difficult to do so. If you do forgive, it seems superficial rather than heart-felt. You recognise you face a crisis of love for that person; you still keep a record of the wrong in your heart.

Sometimes you feel justified in your attitude, that it should not be too easy for others to receive your forgiveness because of the serious nature of the way they have sinned against you. It is as well I don't adopt such an attitude when you need forgiveness from me, isn't it? **I don't make you work for forgiveness, neither do I wait until you deserve it!**

I know it is difficult to maintain love for those who abuse your love and trust again and again. You need to forgive for your own sake as well as for the benefit of the offender. What good does it do to withhold that forgiveness? You only seethe with inward anger and become bitter and resentful. Those attitudes then affect other relationships.

If you forgive too easily you fear this will make you vulnerable to further hurt. What is the alternative? Consider how vulnerable I make myself. When I sent my Son, he was continually abused and rejected. Even those closest to him failed him, deserted and denied him. **Yet in his love he forgave, and forgave, and forgave.**

My Spirit lives within my children. Again and again he is ignored and grieved by their actions. Yet I don't withdraw my presence or stop loving, even when they go through periods of disobedience and rebellion.

How often are you to forgive your brother? Seventy times seven! Yes, if the same one sins against you seven times in a single day, you are still to forgive him seven times, keeping no record of the wrong! If you do this you will maintain your peace and I will be pleased.

Beloved, I have no record of your wrongs; they are washed away completely and for ever through the

love of my Son who gave his life for you! Isn't that a relief!

1 Cor. 13:4–5; Rom. 4:7–8; Matt. 18:21–2; Col. 3:12–14; 1 John 1:9.

71

Love Does Not Delight in Evil

———— o ————

"Let us throw off everything that hinders and the sin that so easily entangles, and let us run with perseverance the race marked out for us."

(Heb. 12:1)

Child, I am glad that you love me. I want you to love what I love, therefore, and to hate what I hate. Jesus was a man of such joy because he loved righteousness and hated every form of evil.

Love does not delight in evil; so I don't want you to delight in any form of evil. You have turned away from many wrong things, but I see that certain forms of sin still attract you. In some areas you would prefer your own ways to mine.

Sin is deceptive. It offers short-term pleasure which if indulged will lead to long-term disaster. Better to walk in the Spirit than in the flesh, for my Spirit brings you life and peace.

But I leave the choice to you; **I never force you to obey me.** Sometimes you wish I would! That would not be love. You would soon resent having to do what I made you do. **And I am not blessed by any other response from my children than one of love.** Their obedience must be willing, an expression of love for me.

Once again I show you how patient I am. My Spirit is at work within you, changing your values. He encourages you in what is good and right, and warns you against those things which grieve me. Take heed of those warnings. **You can be sure that whatever grieves me will not do you any good either!** Better to please me, walk in my ways and enjoy my peace.

And know this, beloved. When there is a particular temptation which seems to afflict you again and again, this is because you don't hate that particular sin. You may hate yourself for your weakness and vulnerability in that area; but you don't yet hate the sin. When you do, it will hold no further attraction for you.

1 Cor. 13:4–7; 2 Tim. 2:22; Rom. 8:10; Rom. 8:6; 1 Pet. 2:24; 1 John 3:9.

72

Love Rejoices in the Truth

———— o ————

"If you hold to my teaching, you are really my disciples. Then you will know the truth and the truth will set you free."

(John 8:31–2)

Beloved, love rejoices in the truth, even when the truth is uncomfortable. And it is sometimes, isn't it, child? There are many aspects of my word you like to avoid. You would like to think that I am not really talking to you in those passages; so you quickly find others which are more acceptable and encouraging. I understand this.

I encourage you with the things you are able to receive and understand now. I don't expect instant perfection. But my Spirit is guiding you into **ALL** the truth; so he will confront you with other aspects of the truth you need to face. He will do this in the right way at the right time.

All scripture is the source of revelation you need in order to understand me and my ways. Treat what I say with reverence and respect. Know that when your views conflict with what I reveal, it is your views which must change.

Jesus is the Bread of Life. I am bringing you to the point where you enjoy the whole diet he offers! In feeding on my word you feed on Jesus, on the truth that sets you free from bondage and builds faith to enable you to face every situation.

Already you rejoice in much of the truth:

You know you are forgiven – that truth is revealed to you through my word.

You know I accept you – that is the truth of my word.

You are a new creation – the old has gone, the new has come.

You are a child of my Kingdom.

You possess eternal life.

I have blessed you in Jesus with every spiritual blessing in heaven.

I always lead you in triumph because you live in Jesus.

I will meet every need you have through his glorious riches.

I have given you everything you need for life and godliness.

My Spirit lives in you.

I have given you fullness of life in Jesus.

All these are truths revealed in my word and you rejoice in them. The more you believe the revelation of my word the more your experience will come into line with the truth.

John 16:13; 2 Tim. 3:16; Eph. 1:3; 2 Pet. 1:3; 2 Cor. 2:14.

73

Love Protects

———— ° ————

"It always protects."

(1 Cor. 13:7)

L ove always protects. My love is a shield about you. I am protective towards you because you are my child. I am your Refuge and Stronghold, I am your Rock, your Fortress and Deliverer.

You protect those you love, especially those for whom you are responsible. Loving parents are protective towards their children. How much more, therefore, will I be protective towards my loved ones.

Children can place themselves in positions of danger through foolishness or ignorance, or by ignoring the warnings they have received. So it is with my children. **While they trust in my word and walk in my ways they are safe.** As soon as they step out of obedience to my word, they make themselves vulnerable.

There have been a number of occasions when I have kept you from your own foolishness. I have prevented the enemy from inflicting harm on you. It has been apparent to you that I have intervened supernaturally to alter the course of events.

The enemy prowls around like a roaring lion seeking those he can devour. As you walk on the highway of holiness you are safe. But if you wander away from me, the enemy will seek to take advantage of you. The number of times I have had to rescue you!

Notice how Jesus was protected from the evil others wanted to inflict on him. On several occasions they would have killed him. But none of those in the control of the enemy could touch him because he lived in close fellowship with me. He lived according to my will.

It was only possible for him to be arrested when he willingly submitted to this and his ensuing crucifixion. He could have summoned legions of angels to his help and protection. He refused to do that because he knew the hour of his sacrifice had come.

Walk close to me, to the truth of my word, and enjoy my protection. And protect those I give you to love. Don't criticise them; be prepared to defend them when others judge them. Warn those who are in danger of grieving me and encourage the fearful to put their trust in my protecting love.

1 Cor. 13:1–13; Ps. 18:30; 1 Pet. 5:8–9; 1 John 5:18.

74

Love Always Trusts

———— ° ————

"It . . . always trusts."

(1 Cor. 13:7)

My dear child, love always trusts. You are learning to trust me in every situation as your love for me grows stronger. You are discovering that when you trust in my words you don't fail and you see my promises fulfilled.

Again and again I tell you not to fear. When you fear you doubt my love for you; my perfect love casts out all fear. Jesus said: **"Do not let your hearts be troubled. Trust in God, trust also in me."**

My love for you is consistent, child. It is dependable and reliable. It doesn't change with your feelings and circumstances. **It is an eternal, unchanging, steadfast love.** And this is the love and faith I am encouraging in you; that your faith in my love will be strong, even when you are in the middle of great difficulties.

The mistake many make is to believe in a general sense without believing specifically what I promise. I am faithful to my words of promise. You doubt my love when you doubt what I say. **Holding on to my words of promise is like holding on to me and my love for you.**

My love abounds to those who call on me. "Whatever you ask in prayer, believe that you have received it and it will be yours." There are times when you have to walk in thanksgiving that you have received the answer you need, even when there is nothing to show for your confidence. You simply know that I will prove faithful in the situation, that what I have promised shall surely happen.

When you pray with faith you are sure I have heard you, and so certain of my answer that you believe you have received.

Beloved, you are blessed because you have put your trust and confidence in me. I will not fail you. I will keep you from falling. Because I am at your right hand, you will not be shaken!

I will bring you to the fulfilment of all I have planned for you. Trust me.

1 Cor. 13:1–13; 1 John 4:18; John 14:1; Mark 11:24; Heb. 11:1.

75

Love Hopes

———— o ————

"It . . . always hopes."

(1 Cor. 13:7)

Love always hopes. My dear child, my eyes are on those who hope in my unfailing love; they will never be put to shame.

Faith is being sure of what you hope for in the future. There is no doubt that I will do what I have said I will do. **I see you already seated in heavenly places in Jesus; he will present you spotless and blameless before me.**

Because there is nothing or no one imperfect in heaven, you needed a Saviour, someone who could make you perfect in my sight. I don't see you apart from Jesus but living in him! He is your righteousness.

That is not the way you feel, is it? You are aware that at times you have unrighteous desires and yield to temptation. Your actions are not always pleasing to me. So it still seems odd that I should regard you as holy, and assure you that your place in heaven is guaranteed!

Your hope is secure. **I have promised that Jesus will come again and he will. I have promised you will know my glory and you will. I have promised to sanctify you through and through, spirit, soul and body; and I will.**

I have promised you will shine like the sun in my Kingdom; and you will! I have spoken!

There is nothing uncertain about your hope; it shall be as I have said it shall be. **"Hope that is seen is no hope at all. Who hopes for what he already has? But if we hope for what we do not yet have, we wait for it patiently."**

My love for you will bring you to the fulfilment of your hope. Hope does not disappoint. This is in stark contrast to the world's concept of hope, which is vague and uncertain. To the non-believer hope is a large question mark. He hopes the future will be good, but is far from sure.

There are those who hope I will answer their prayer, or heal their sickness, but this is a long way short of the assurance faith gives.

Your faith enables you to be sure of what you hope for. So rejoice, beloved. I am the God of hope who fills you with all joy and peace as you trust in me, so that you may overflow with hope by the power of the Holy Spirit.

You will persevere in love, faith and hope – the qualities that will never end!

1 Cor. 13:1–13; Ps. 25:3,5; Ps. 31:24; Ps. 33:18,22; Ps. 62:5; Heb. 11:1; Rom. 8:24–5; Rom. 15:13.

76

Love Never Fails

———— o ————

"It . . . always perseveres. Love never fails."
(1 Cor. 13:7–8)

I have persevered in my love for you, haven't I? I have brought you through every struggle and dilemma, every period of doubt, even when you despaired of yourself and your situation. I never give up on those I love! **I will never give up on you, beloved; you are too precious to me.** My love for you is eternal and it will never fail!

It is encouraging to see the ways in which you persevere because you love me. You have resisted the temptation to forsake my ways. You are learning that it is better to please me than to please yourself. You are having to persist even though sometimes you fail again and again.

Some lessons take more time than others to become reality in your life, don't they? I have to repeat myself until you are prepared to take what I say seriously. But I persevere, gently and lovingly prompting you into action.

My love will never fail you, no matter what struggles you experience or difficulties you have to face. Even when you wander from my ways, I am always there when you return, ready to forgive and restore you. My love will always measure up to your need.

This same love has been placed in you. Yes, you have within you the love that never fails, the love of my Holy Spirit. Know, therefore, that you have the resources of love to cope with any situation.

Others need to know that you will persevere in your love for them, even though they fail you. Yes, there will be times of frustration where you will be disappointed at the way others respond to your love or take you for granted. Show them that you will not give up on them.

Emotionally immature people will go to great lengths to test whether your love for them is genuine. They will try to be manipulative, suggesting even that you don't love them at all. Be strong in the face of such tactics. Love them with the truth, not with sentiment.

Beloved, because my Spirit lives in you, it is possible for you to fulfil the new commandment Jesus gave, to love others as he has loved you. **I want you to have the reputation of being reliable, dependable, faithful and caring – like me!**

1 Cor. 13:1–13; 1 Pet. 4:8; Eph. 4:15; 1 Pet. 1:22.

77

Bless at all Times

—— ○ ——

**"Bless those who persecute you; bless and do not curse
. . . Live in harmony with one another."**

(Rom. 12:14,16)

I t is easy to love those who love you, child. I tell you
to love your enemies, do good to those who hate you,
bless those who curse you, pray for those who persecute
you. Some think my teaching impractical and impossible. It is, unless you have the life of my Spirit within
you.

Those who live at the level of their lower nature will
hate their enemies, returning hatred with hatred. Those
who know me exhibit my mercy and grace. My Spirit
gives them the resources with which to meet hatred
with love, curse with blessing and persecution with
prayer.

With my heart you can love even those who oppose
and hate me. Recognise that such people are bound
and don't understand the truth. They have received
neither the revelation nor the life I have given you.
So don't judge them. **Your fight is not against flesh
and blood, but against the powers which bind people;
the rulers, authorities and powers of this dark
world and the spiritual forces of evil in the heavenly
realms.**

Anyone who opposes you opposes me. The one who hates you hates me. The one who persecutes you persecutes me because you are part of Jesus' Body.

On one occasion his disciples wanted to call down fire from heaven in judgment. Who would be saved if I pronounced judgment on people as soon as they sinned? I am the God of infinite patience and give time for repentance; I sweep away their sins when people turn to me. There are many in my Kingdom who once hated me and opposed those who belong to me. Now they are strong in my Spirit and mighty in their witness of my love.

Beloved, show others that my Kingdom is one of love and that I prefer to bless, not curse, to forgive rather than judge. You will be amazed at how many are defeated by such tactics.

Luke 6:27–36; 2 Cor. 4:3–4; Eph. 6:12; 2 Pet. 3:9.

78

Your Worth

———— o ————

"I have summoned you by name; you are mine."
(Isa. 43:1)

Beloved child, you are much more important to me than you realise. You consider yourself one of a great multitude of disciples I have all over the world. This is true, but every one of my children is important to me. **I would not have called you and come to live in you unless I considered you significant.**

You are a unique person with a unique ministry. **Nobody else can be you!** So stop longing to be someone else! I place you in positions where I can work through you. If it was not my purpose to use you, I would have chosen someone else and put them in those places.

I am with you always to enable and protect you. Let me use you where you are; stop longing to be somewhere else! I will make it clear to you when I want you to go elsewhere.

Beloved, all around you there are people to love, encourage and serve. I have given you plenty to do, for I never waste any of my children. So don't waste time analysing yourself; get on with the job I have given you. The life of faith is exciting; you will be amazed at what you will accomplish. And you will discover that the portion I have assigned to you is good! Yes, you have a delightful inheritance; so live in the good of it!

Ps. 139:13–16; Eph. 2:10; 1 Cor. 7:24; Matt. 9:37–8; Ps. 16:5–6.

79

A Heart Full of Love

———— o ————

"Dear friends, since God so loved us, we also ought to love one another."

(1 John 4:11)

Beloved, I took hold of you and put you into Jesus. All my riches and resources became yours. His inheritance became your inheritance. You are a co-heir with him. Such great privileges bring responsibilities. You must share in my suffering if you are to share in my glory, taking up your cross day by day to follow me. Beloved one, it is worth it!

The suffering to which I call you is the cost of living for the sake of my Kingdom. It is costly to deny yourself and to live for others instead. But if your heart is full of love for me it will be full of love for others, and the cost will be outweighed by the sheer joy of seeing what I do in them when you reach out on my behalf.

You know how I have loved you, don't you, child? I gave myself whole-heartedly without holding back. It would not have been enough for me to give part of myself. I gave myself totally, first by becoming man, and then by dying on the cross. I considered it worthwhile because I love you.

If that is how I loved you, that is how you must love others. You please me by serving them.

Are you afraid they will take advantage of your love? They will; just as they take advantage of my love. Do you think they will take your love for granted? They will; just as they have taken my love for granted.

Do you try to take advantage of my love? Do you ever take my love for granted? Realise that others treat you in the same way that you treat me.

I don't condemn you, and it is not your place to condemn them. Warn the disobedient, encourage the faithful.

Keep loving and giving to others even when they don't seem appreciative or thankful. Remember, even Jesus learned obedience from what he suffered, being faithful in giving himself in love, even to the point of death on a cross! **I love because it is my nature to love. I want this to be true of you also, beloved.**

1 John 4:11–12; Rom. 8:17; Matt. 10:38–9.

80

I Will Reward You

———— o ————

**"Whatever you do, work at it with all your heart . . .
since you know that you will receive an inheritance
from the Lord as a reward."**

(Col. 3:23–4)

Y ou can only walk in the plans I have for you if you
live in the revelation of my love. It is not selfish to
expect my blessing and to receive the abundance I want
to give you. **The more you receive, the more you will
have to give to others.**

I would not give to you unless this was what I wanted. Of
course you don't deserve my blessings. I don't give because
you deserve my gifts but because I love you.

You have often found it difficult to understand my
generosity. Do you remember the story Jesus told about
the workers in the vineyard? Some worked in the heat
for a whole day and some only for one hour; but all
were paid the same amount because this was what the
master agreed with each worker.

Some complained because this seemed unjust. Don't
I have the right to do what I want with my own? It is
never unjust for me to do what I have promised!

The person who lives his whole life serving me and
suffering persecution will receive salvation; and so

will the person who turns to me in the latter part of his life.

Those who have worked with me and suffered the heat of the day have known much greater satisfaction than those whose lives had no purpose or significance until the closing hour. **You are blessed to be working with me now.** You are blessed to know me and believe in me, to have my presence with you always. I rejoice in you with great and abundant joy!

Beloved child, **don't concentrate on the cost, but on the joy of knowing that you serve me.** I will reward you. And know that whenever you endure hardship for the sake of my Kingdom, you bless me by your willingness to be a living sacrifice. I assure you of this: you will never be the loser. I am no man's debtor. I will never allow you to out-do me in giving! You will receive from me far more than you could ever give!

Matt. 20:1–16; Eph. 6:7–8; Matt. 16:27.

81

The Fruit of Obedience

———— ○ ————

"This is love for God: to obey his commands."
(1 John 5:3)

Dear child, some lessons are very simple but have
profound consequences in your life. Jesus told of
a father who wanted his two sons to work in his fields.
The first said he would go, but didn't. The other
refused, then thought better of his father's request and
went. Which one did his father's will?

Many say they want to do my will but don't do it. **It
is not the words of commitment that impress me, but
the obedience that bears fruit in positive action.** The
one who loves me will obey my commands.

So, beloved, it is important that you have decided to
do my will, that you want to please me in all things.
Now I am looking for the evidence of what you say, the
fruit of your commitment.

Matt. 21:28–31; John 14:15; Luke 11:28; 2 John 6.

82

I Desire Mercy, Not Sacrifice

——— o ———

"If any one of you is without sin, let him be the first to throw a stone at her."

(John 8:7)

The religious leaders tried to trap Jesus when they brought to him a woman caught in the act of adultery. There was no doubt about her guilt; under the Law she should be stoned to death. Jesus had made it clear that he had come to fulfil the Law, not to do away with it. How could his teaching of love and forgiveness be reconciled with the judgment this woman deserved?

The Pharisees didn't understand that my mercy was at the heart of the law I gave my people. They were concerned about the outward performance of religious duties, but missed my heart!

Although Jesus never condoned sin, he loved sinners and used every opportunity to set them free from their sins. "If any one of you is without sin, let him be the first to throw a stone at her." The only sinless one present was Jesus. He chose to forgive the woman, not throw stones at her. **I prefer mercy to judgment!**

The mood of the crowd changed. The oldest and wisest were the first to drift away. How could they judge this woman when Jesus could reveal the sins of everyone there if he chose to do so?

"Doesn't anyone condemn you?" he asked the woman. "No one," she said. So Jesus sent her away and told her to leave her life of sin. Do you think she did?

Learn this lesson well, beloved. When tempted to judge and condemn others, remember your own need for mercy.

John 8:1–11; Jas. 2:12–13; Matt. 9:13; Luke 6:37.

83

The Pharisees

———— ० ————

"These people honour me with their lips, but their hearts are far from me. They worship me in vain; their teachings are but rules taught by men."

(Mark 7:6–7)

Beloved, have nothing to do with the leaven of the Pharisees. They are full of good advice, but don't live by their own teaching. They are full of self-righteousness and oppose my purposes, even though they pay me lip-service. They don't live as the children of my Kingdom. Some even oppose the new birth saying this is not necessary to inherit my Kingdom, in direct contradiction to the truth Jesus proclaims.

The Pharisees are those who want others to follow after them, to acknowledge and acclaim them. They are more concerned about their status and position than the welfare of my children.

The Pharisees are those who are concerned about commitment, but to the things they consider dear, not to the things I count sacred. They are blind, preferring their own "wisdom" to my truth.

The Pharisees are those who are meticulous about their church law and denominational constitutions, but leave my children languishing in their need of life and healing. They neglect the justice, mercy, and faithfulness which are evidences of the presence of my Kingdom in their midst. This is another indication of their blindness. They fuss about details but ignore the important principles of my Kingdom.

The Pharisees clean the outside of the cup, but are full of greed and self-indulgence on the inside. They are concerned about their appearance before others, but fail to realise that their hearts are an open book to me. Inwardly they are full of corruption. They don't recognise their hypocrisy and so they don't cry out to me for the clean hearts they need.

They honour past traditions and exalt former teachers, but neglect my word. They read the scriptures but fail to bring their lives into line with what I say. They even oppose and persecute those who do live by faith, accusing them of arrogance.

Beware of such people. My Spirit cannot move freely where such pharisaism is allowed to rule. **By contrast, wherever my Spirit is allowed to rule there will be freedom among my people.**

Child, you don't belong among the Pharisees. You are called to live the life of my Kingdom in the power of my Spirit, and I want you to be free to do so. **You are not to be under those who judge you, but submitted to those who will genuinely lead you in my ways; men and women of faith and vision who will teach you my word and encourage your faith.**

Matt. 15:1–9; Matt. 23:23–8; 1 Sam. 16:7; 2 Cor. 3:17; 1 Cor. 4:20.

84

My Spirit Gives Life

———— o ————

**"Not everyone who says to me, 'Lord, Lord, will enter
the kingdom of heaven, but only he who does the will
of my Father who is in heaven."**

(Matt. 7:21)

W oe to you, Pharisees! That is still my word. There
are many modern-day Pharisees who are content
with the outward form of religion, but lack the inner
reality of my Spirit. They practise their formalities of
worship and hold on to their traditions with sincerity;
yet there is no power either in their own lives or the
lives of those they teach. In fact, some try to prevent
others from receiving the power I want to pour into
their lives.

Even though the Pharisees were leading members of
the synagogue, Jesus warned them that they would not
enter the Kingdom of heaven. Sinners and prostitutes
were being received into the Kingdom ahead of them,
because they were turning to me with repentance and
faith.

Some today will not acknowledge their need of
repentance, but are content with their ritual forms of
religion. They believe I am Lord, but have no experience
of new birth because they are not personally submitted
to my Lordship. They claim to have received my Spirit,
although there is no evidence of my power in their lives.

They resent people asking them if they are born again, and become very defensive when challenged about their personal relationship with me.

Those who know me have no need to be defensive. They rejoice in the relationship we enjoy together. They know the reality of my Spirit working in them.

I warn those who wash the outside of the dish but inwardly their hearts are corrupt. I warn those who persist in things I consider detestable: occult practices, superstition and homosexuality. They shall not know me now or eternally unless they yield their lives to me and allow me to work the changes in them that I am able to perform.

I shall call to account all those who teach in my name. They have a double responsibility. **Those who teach the truth and lead my people into the truth shall have a double reward.** Those who promote their own rational ideas and opinions have on their hands the blood of those for whom they are responsible.

Those who bring their thoughts and actions into line with what I teach are those who truly follow me. Their joy shall be full and they shall be satisfied and fulfilled. They will be free themselves and can deliver others from bondage through speaking my truth into their lives. Those who receive the truth through them shall rejoice.

Beloved, pray for those who teach and lead my people, that they will prove faithful to me.

Matt. 15:8–9; Jas. 3:1; Matt. 21:31.

85

My Justice

———— o ————

"Do not judge, or you too will be judged . . . with the measure you use, it will be measured to you."
(Matt. 7:1–2)

I warn you not to judge others, for you will be judged by the same standards you impose on others. I don't tell you to judge the "Pharisees" and those who oppose me. I tell you to beware of them and what they teach, to have nothing to do with lifeless religion. I alone have the right to judge.

I am just. I ensure that you will be treated justly and I will deal with everyone else with justice. **You will reap what you sow. So treat others in the way you want them to treat you.** Be merciful and you will receive my mercy.

Sometimes your love is rejected, your gifts spurned. If those to whom you give do not respond, I will ensure that others give back to you. This is my way. I oversee all the details of your life to ensure my justice prevails for you.

When others treat you unjustly you don't have to retaliate or seek revenge. I will cause justice to be done. I will deal with those who oppress you. Either they will repent and know my mercy, or they will be judged, for those who oppose you, oppose me.

I always vindicate righteousness, even if this seems to take time. You are very pleased when I give you time to repent. **Be equally thankful that I give others time to repent.** Ensure that you are as patient with others as I am with you.

Keep your heart attitudes pure – free from jealousy and bitterness, lust and greed. Be as concerned for the welfare of others as you are about your own welfare. Love those who despise and hate you. Remember how hard their hearts must be to hate those whom I love, and oppress those I affirm.

Do these things seem too hard for you, child? Ask my Spirit to help you. You have his life and you are able to do whatever I ask of you.

Matt. 7:1–6; Matt. 26:52; Phil. 2:3–4; Luke 6:37–42.

86

Forgive

———— o ————

"Shouldn't you have had mercy on your fellow-servant just as I had on you?"

(Matt. 18:33)

J esus told the parable of the unmerciful servant to show how my forgiveness operates. The servant had his huge debt cancelled by the master, but then refused to forgive the paltry debt he was owed by a fellow-servant. He had him thrown into prison because he couldn't repay the debt. The master was angry with the wicked servant, called him to account and handed him over to the jailers to be tortured until he could pay back all he owed.

You bless me, beloved, whenever you are merciful; you grieve me when you refuse to forgive. Because you have experienced my mercy yourself I expect you to be merciful to others. When you refuse to be merciful, you can no longer experience my mercy. The measure you give is the measure you get back.

Blessed are the merciful for they have obtained mercy. Forgive and you will be forgiven. Do not judge, or you too will be judged. For in the same way you judge others, you will be judged, and with the measure you use, it will be measured to you.

I never want to withdraw my mercy from any of my children. Yet the matter of forgiveness is so important to me this is what I do when they harden their hearts against others. Those who are forgiven much, love much. And their love is expressed in showing mercy and forgiveness to others.

Sometimes you struggle to forgive others because you have been hurt by the unjust ways in which they have dealt with you. It is even more difficult when it seems they are unrepentant! It will help you to remember how thoroughly I have forgiven you in the past without judging or condemning you. Realise how much your sin has offended me, and be thankful for my mercy; then you will be able to forgive others from your heart.

And don't lose patience, child. You will have to forgive some people again and again – just as I have had to forgive you repeatedly. **I am only asking you to treat others in the same way that I treat you; with love, mercy and grace.**

Matt. 18:21–35; Matt. 5:7; Matt. 6:14–15.

87

I Am Just

———— ο ————

"If I do judge, my decisions are right, because I am not alone. I stand with the Father, who sent me."

(John 8:16)

My dear child, I entrusted all judgment to my Son so that everyone may honour him as they honour me. We are one, yet distinctive in personality. We are not at odds with each other, but always work in perfect harmony. Although all judgment is entrusted to Jesus, he judges only as he hears. His judgments are my judgments, and they are always just.

I was able to entrust everything to my Son, even in the days when he shared the weakness of your humanity, because he did not seek to please himself.

And my Spirit gives you a right spiritual judgment or assessment of every situation in which you are placed. So listen carefully to the inner witness of my Spirit so that you are not deceived. **Because you live in me you share my capacity to judge; you are able to distinguish between the things which glorify me and those which dishonour me.**

You can discern what spirits are at work because my Holy Spirit gives you such discernment. You are able to determine if someone is operating in the flesh or under an anointing from me; or whether he is being used by the enemy. You are not standing in judgment on people, but coming to a right understanding of the spirit behind their words and actions. You are to "judge" in that sense.

Because you believe in Jesus he will not judge and accuse you before me but will speak in your defence. He is your Advocate. His blood speaks for you, beloved. I am just in refusing to judge and condemn you because you have put your trust in the sacrifice he has made for you on the cross. I will never deny the blood of my Son. You are cleansed by that blood. Rejoice! You will not be condemned, but have already passed from death to life!

1 John 2:1; John 5:22; 1 Cor. 2:15; Rom. 5:9; John 5:24.

88

My Judgment

———— o ————

**"For he has set a day when he will judge the world
with justice by the man he has appointed."**

(Acts 17:31)

B eloved, the time will come when all will come before
my seat of judgment. Those who refuse to believe
in Jesus are condemned already. They are right to fear
the Day of Judgment. They have rejected the blood that
has the power to cleanse them from their sin and make
them acceptable in my sight. No one can speak for
them. They are condemned by their unbelief.

**Those who are mine have nothing to fear. Jesus'
blood speaks for them. They are saved.**

All my children will have to give account for the way
they have used the resources of my Kingdom which I
have made available to them. Each will receive the
reward appropriate to his or her actions. The faithful
and obedient will have a different reward from those
who have lived to please themselves. Live in such a way
as to win praise from me.

At the judgment, the sheep shall be separated from
the goats. I regard those who do my will as members
of my family. They are the sheep who follow me. The
goats do not reach out to others in my name.

Those who are filled with my love are sometimes not even conscious of the way they co-operate with me; it has become their nature to allow my life to flow through them. They love others instinctively and they give without stopping to consider the cost to themselves.

When these righteous ones come before my throne, I will commend them for the way they have satisfied the hungry and thirsty, entertained strangers, clothed the naked, cared for the sick and visited those in prison. Many of them will be astonished that I should commend them for such things because this has seemed so natural for them. They have not been motivated by expectation of reward; they have acted with hearts filled with genuine compassion and love. **They have ministered to me by ministering to others. It is my pleasure to reward them.**

Others who have done none of these things will say they love me, but will have produced little or no fruit. These are the people who want to use me, not serve me; so they use others for their own purposes instead of serving them. They call me "Lord" but do not allow me to be Lord. Not everyone who says, "Lord, Lord" will enter the Kingdom of heaven, but only he who does what I say.

Beloved, I rejoice that you are among the sheep. You hear my voice and follow me. You reach out to others with my love. You touch their lives where they hurt. Instead of condemning them, you love them.

Matt. 25:31–46; Rom. 14:10–12; John 3:18; Matt. 16:27; Matt. 7:21.

89

Your King and Judge

———— o ————

"The whole crowd of disciples began joyfully to praise God in loud voices . . . Blessed is the king who comes in the name of the Lord!"

(Luke 19:37–8)

Jesus wept over Jerusalem. He had given my people many opportunities to believe the good news and turn to me in repentance. Many preferred their religion to my Son, and yet professed faith in me as their Father.

Many do the same today. I am not pleased with external rituals or the outward display of formal religion. I want a people whose hearts are on fire for me and the cause of my Kingdom; those who live as my witnesses and have a longing to see the lost saved.

Jesus wept over Jerusalem. This should have been the place where he was received as the Messiah, the Christ, my Son. Instead it was the place of his rejection. Does not the same thing happen today? The greatest opposition to the truth is among those you imagine would welcome my word and have hearts to do my will!

Some in Jerusalem greeted him as King when he entered the city in triumph on a donkey, the symbol of kingship. The people recognised him as the Son of David, that he came in my name as their King. Most of the religious leaders didn't raise their voices in acclamation. Instead they conspired together against him.

When he comes again in triumph, he will not be judged by religious leaders or anyone else; he will judge all men. He will come as both King and Judge.

But this was the time for the King to lay aside his kingly robes and submit himself to every indignity man could heap upon him. Voices would soon be raised demanding his crucifixion instead of proclaiming his kingship. The powers of darkness and formal religion would seem to have their way, but only momentarily. **For the King was on the way to his throne. He came by way of the cross so that he could bring you to heaven with him.**

Beloved, I am so pleased that your voice is among those raised in acclamation, proclaiming Jesus as your King and Lord. Let his praise be continually on your lips. Enter my gates with thanksgiving; come into my courts with praise. Praise the name of Jesus, for you shall praise him eternally:

"Worthy is the Lamb, who was slain, to receive power and wealth and wisdom and strength and honour and glory and praise!"

Matt. 23:37; Matt. 23:1–36; Acts 17:31; Rev. 5:12.

90

I Restore You

———— o ————

"If we confess our sins, he is faithful and just and will forgive us our sins and purify us from all unrighteousness."

(1 John 1:9)

Jesus knew it would happen. He knew through whom it would happen; yet he never allowed this knowledge to colour his dealings with Judas. He gave him the same opportunities as all the other disciples; he loved him with the same love and treated him with the same grace.

He gave Judas every opportunity to respond to his love; but Judas was typical of those who want their reward now. He wanted his political ambitions and worldly greed fulfilled. He saw himself as the social reformer, not a man of the Spirit. He expected of others standards by which he didn't want to live himself.

Jesus was not the kind of Messiah Judas wanted! Yet Jesus' heart was heavy for Judas when he betrayed him. Don't you grieve, beloved, for those in the grip of the devil, being manipulated and used by him?

Many have questioned why one so close to Jesus should be the one to betray him. Isn't that always the way? Opposition from outside the number of believers strengthens their faith and resolve. Betrayal within the Church causes the greatest damage.

After Judas had betrayed Jesus, he was full of remorse but was not repentant. He had sided with Satan; he had served the enemy's purposes and the devil destroys those who are his. Let this be a warning to everyone.

Peter denied Jesus. He was truly repentant. His love for Jesus was genuine and was not based on self-interest. So he was restored and given the commission to feed my sheep. His ministry became a great blessing to many people.

Some of my servants deny me by the things they do and say. When they realise what they have done, they are truly sorry and repent. **You are to reinstate such brothers, not judge or condemn them.**

I didn't shut Peter out of my purposes, or say he was no longer worthy to feed my people because he deserted and then denied me. I restored him and commissioned him. When my Spirit came on the disciples it was Peter who took the lead preaching my word and initiating the move that led to thousands turning to me in faith.

Understand, child, that your past failures once forgiven are forgotten by me. I don't allow them to hinder the ways I will use you in the future. This is another aspect of my mercy!

John 13:10–11; John 18:15–17, 25–7; John 21:15–17; Ps. 103:12.

91

The Hour of Glory

——— o ———

"He humbled himself and became obedient to death –
even death on a cross!"

(Phil. 2:8)

The moment had come and the disciples fled leaving
Jesus alone. Now he sat before the courts of men –
Caiaphas, Annas, Pilate. He heard the wild accusations
ranged against him. He listened to the hatred and the
total lack of understanding.

He had denounced the authorities, the Sadducees
and Herodians who had refused to believe his words.
Judgment was already passed upon them. Now Jesus
listened to their judgment concerning their Messiah.
They wanted to put to death the One who was sent to
deliver them from the law of death. They were more
in love with their tradition than with me. They didn't
recognise the One I sent. How I grieved for them!

My purpose had to be fulfilled. Jesus had nothing to
say to those wild and false accusations. He would not
defend himself. Before long I would vindicate him by
raising him from the dead. Then the truth would be
seen for who he is!

When Jesus was directly challenged as to whether he
was the Christ, he proclaimed, "I am". Those who loved
him recognised the impact of such a statement. Those

who rejected him accused him of blasphemy. They chose to crucify him!

Earlier, Jesus had called these same religious leaders the children of the devil. Now they were seen to be just that. Despite their claims to righteousness and obedience to the law they were instruments in the devil's hand being used to crucify my Son.

I know who the true children of God are. They love Jesus and honour my word. The children of the devil prefer reason to truth, religion to love and argument to power. Jesus had to stand in the weakness of his humanity and allow them to judge him.

The sentence was swift. Little did they realise that this was the hour of my glory when I would fulfil perfectly my reasons for sending Jesus. When they whipped and beat him, he said nothing. He allowed sin and sickness to be laid on him. All the pain that men deserve was cast on him. He bore it willingly. He knew the end of these things would culminate in victory, but he still had to endure the pain and agony.

What did Jesus feel as they banged the nails through his hands and feet? **He prayed for you, child, and for all who made his death necessary: "Father, forgive them, they don't know what they are doing."**

John 8:42–7; Matt. 27:27–54; Col. 2:13–15.

92

Jesus, Your Sacrifice

———— ∘ ————

"It is finished."

(John 19:30)

Dear beloved one, as Jesus knelt in the garden that night I saw his anguish of soul. Yet I had to be unrelenting in my purpose. I heard him pray the words, "Not my will but yours be done"; and I confirmed to him that my will was to send him to the cross.

I saw the beating, the mocking and spitting. I heard the lies of those who gave testimony against him; but I knew also of the multitudes who in the future would be testifying for him because of his obedience. I saw the nails driven into his hands and feet. I heard the cry of anguish: "My God, my God! Why have you forsaken me?"

The most difficult thing I have ever had to do was to leave him to suffer utterly alone. **I could not be part of that suffering because it was for my sake that he hung there. The justice of my wrath was turned from people and placed on him. He had to suffer the punishment they deserved.** As I listened to the cry of desperation he was cut off from me. Yet this was the only sacrifice that could set men free: the perfect offering of himself for the imperfect, the selfless giving himself on behalf of the selfish, the righteous delivered to death for the unrighteous. Such an event would never have to be repeated.

I saw the triumph of faith as he hung there. Even though he knew the utter desolation of being separated from me, he committed his Spirit into my care. At that time he had no sense of my presence. It was an act of sheer faith and I rejoiced for him.

Seeing my Son suffer in this way brought me both joy and sorrow. The sorrow of separation was necessary to enable the joy that would come because of the harvest of souls which would subsequently be birthed into my Kingdom.

"It is finished," he cried in triumph. Everything I sent him to do to secure your salvation was accomplished. The spotless Lamb was offered in sacrifice for the sins of the whole world.

His body was taken down from the cross and laid lifeless in the tomb. Having preached to the imprisoned spirits, he could demonstrate his triumphant resurrection and victory over death.

Dear child, you believe that he died for you and so all the virtue of the cross is yours: forgiveness, healing, freedom. You believe in his resurrection, so you, too, will be raised and will reign triumphantly with me in heaven. Never forget that, child! And know that **because I love you so much, I consider it worthwhile to have paid such a high price for you. You are so precious to me!**

Matt. 26:36–27:66; Isa. 53:5; Heb. 7:24–7; Rom. 6:5.

93

Believe My Word

——— o ———

"But blessed are your eyes because they see, and your ears because they hear."

(Matt. 13:16)

They didn't understand. Although Jesus warned the disciples on several occasions, they didn't believe what he said. It was foreign to their expectations and to everything they wanted of their Messiah. They couldn't understand why the Son of God had to be rejected and crucified. The thought was so appalling, they never received the promise in their hearts that he would be raised again. So after the crucifixion they hid in fear, feeling utterly devastated by what had happened.

When told by those who had gone to the tomb that Jesus had risen, they wouldn't believe it. Not until they saw the risen Jesus themselves did they believe.

When he appeared to the disciples Thomas was absent; he refused to believe the others' testimony until he had seen for himself.

What does all this prove? Unbelief is very powerful. Many people receive revelation of the truth but meet it with unbelief.

Do you remember what Jesus said to Thomas? "You believe because you have seen. Blessed are those who believe though they have not seen." You have not seen Jesus in the flesh, have you, child? So, beloved, **you are one of my blessed ones. You believe though you have not seen.**

Because you believed the testimony of my word you know the truth and the truth has set you free! You realise that **I do not treat you as you deserve, but as he deserves.** He has borne the punishment you deserved.

Only those who repent and trust in his redeeming love are able to enjoy the benefits of his sacrifice.

A store can be filled with all manner of goods; yet many choose to pass by that store. They may admire the goods from a distance or ignore the store altogether. Only those who enter and purchase the goods can enjoy them.

This does not imply you can buy my gifts; but you do have to enter in by faith in order to receive them. There is a store full of spiritual wealth, and everything is already paid for by the blood of my Son.

Many choose to pass by and ignore what I offer. Beloved, **I am so pleased that you have come to me to receive what I freely give through Jesus.**

You have received salvation, eternal life, the Kingdom of heaven and all my other riches because you believed my word! That is the power of faith.

Dear child, continue to enter in and receive all that I offer you through my Son.

John 20:24–9; Eph. 1:13; Eph. 1:18–21.

94

The Lamb Now Reigns

—— o ——

"Therefore he is able to save completely those who come to God through him, because he always lives to intercede for them . . . He sacrificed for their sins once for all when he offered himself."

(Heb. 7:25,27)

Behold the Lamb of God who takes away the sin of the world! Behold my Son, sent to be your sacrifice. The Lamb without blemish, the holy offering made to the holy God to atone for all the sins of the unholy. Look at the Lamb who has taken away **your** sin.

Behold the Lamb of God now in the midst of the throne, reigning in heaven. He has opened the way for you to come into the Holy of Holies with a sincere heart and in full assurance of faith. When he died on the cross, the veil of the temple was torn in two. **Now there is nothing to prevent you from coming into the inner courts of my kingly presence.** There you can hear and receive from me.

You don't have to speak to me from a distance. Come into the Holy of Holies. Worship before my throne. Stand in the courts of praise. Know that you are welcome because you acknowledge me as Lord and King. This is where you belong.

You enter this place briefly through prayer and worship. The time will come, beloved, when I will raise you to that place of glory for all eternity. This is my promise. You only have fleeting glimpses of my glory now; then you shall see me face to face. Now you know I am the light; then you will enjoy that light eternally. Now you have but an impression of the power of my majesty; then you will enjoy my kingly rule for ever.

I am he who reigns in glory, and yet is with you to help and encourage you. **You were in Jesus when he was sacrificed on the cross; and you were in him as he was raised to glory.** You live in the Glorious One who has shared your humanity and has overcome every evil.

I see you seated in heavenly places already. He has prepared your place for you. I have given you my Holy Spirit, and he is the guarantee of your inheritance which is to come.

Behold, the Lamb of God who takes away your sin. Behold the Lamb enthroned in heavenly glory.

Rev. 7:9–17; Heb. 10:19–22; 2 Cor. 5:5; 1 Cor. 13:12.

95

Rejoice In Me

———— o ————

"Lord, to whom shall we go? You have the words of eternal life."

(John 6:68)

Jesus rejoiced to do my will even though he had to suffer so much opposition, rejection and even crucifixion. He rejoiced in being obedient because he loved me.

The cross was like a shadow over his life. He could not avoid it. There was no other way to fulfil my purpose of salvation. Throughout his life he had resisted every temptation to sin. He had overcome every device of the enemy. He had been victorious throughout, and then had to allow himself to be falsely accused, judged, condemned and crucified.

He took on himself all the sin he had so carefully avoided and had to experience its terrible consequences. **He went through the darkness of the cross so you could have light.** The darkness could not overcome him.

Sometimes everything seems dark to you, doesn't it? You have no sense of my light or my presence. Yet I have not deserted you and I hear your cry for help. I will lead you through the darkness into light. You will not be overcome by the problem.

Here in heaven Jesus is your Advocate. He speaks on your behalf. His blood speaks louder than your sin. His victory transcends all your failure. His love obliterates all your fear.

He will intercede for you until your appointed time comes; then you will be with me in glory for ever.

So, beloved child, rejoice in the work I have done for you through the cross. Be thankful to Jesus for this sacrifice. **You have been crucified with Christ. It is no longer you who lives, but Christ in you. The life you now live in the body you live by faith in the Son of God who loves you and gave his life for you.**

John 12:46; Ps. 139:11–12; John 1:1–2; Gal. 2:20.

96

The Resurrection

———— o ————

"For my Father's will is that everyone who looks to the Son and believes in him shall have eternal life, and I will raise him up at the last day."

(John 6:40)

T he Lamb that made his life a sacrifice for sin has risen triumphantly and reigns! Death could not hold him.

Neither will death be able to hold those who put their trust in him. **Death cannot hold you, child, for you have put your trust in the One who is the Resurrection.** He is eternal life and you have received that life through him. Whoever lives and believes in him will never die eternally. You believe this, don't you?

So you can enjoy the fullness of his life now, and also have the security of knowing your eternal destiny is assured.

The tomb could not hold Jesus. The same body that hung on the cross was raised, and Jesus appeared to his disciples in his risen body on a number of occasions.

You too, child, will have a bodily resurrection. You don't need to speculate as to what this will mean. Believe it as the revelation of truth. I have made it clear that when Jesus was raised he was the firstfruits of those who had fallen asleep in death. All who live in Christ shall be made alive in him. As the firstfruit has been raised, so shall all who belong to him also be raised.

Jesus shall reign until he has put all his enemies under his feet. And the last enemy to be destroyed is death.

Your perishable body will be raised imperishable. That which was sown in dishonour will be raised in glory; that which was sown in weakness will be raised in power. It is now a natural body but it will be raised a spiritual body.

You cannot imagine what that means, neither is it wise to speculate. The host of heaven are spiritual beings and each has a spiritual body. And you will take your place before my throne in your spiritual body. Yes, that natural body will become a spiritual body.

All you need to know now about your spiritual body is this: **it will bear the likeness of Jesus!** Yes, beloved, you will be changed in a flash, in the twinkling of an eye, when the last trumpet sounds. **You will be raised imperishable; your mortal life will be clothed with immortality. Then the saying that is written will come true: "Death has been swallowed up in victory!"**

John 11:26; 1 Cor. 15:20–3, 42–3; 1 Cor. 15:54.

97

Receive My Body and Blood

———— o ————

"For my flesh is real food and my blood is real drink. Whoever eats my flesh and drinks my blood remains in me, and I in him."

(John 6:55–6)

M eanwhile, beloved, you are called to live my life in the weakness of your human body, not depending on your own frail resources but on the life of Jesus.

On the night he was arrested, he took bread, broke it and gave thanks to me saying: **"This is my body which is given for you."** Every time they broke bread together, Jesus wanted his disciples to remember that he gave himself whole-heartedly to them. They have his strength to sustain them physically.

He took the cup, gave thanks and gave it to the disciples saying: **"This is my blood of the new covenant, shed for you and for many for the forgiveness of sins."** He told them to do this to remember him. They could live continually in my mercy, knowing that I forgive all their sins and failure.

It was not my intention for men to make this into a formal service. I want you and all my children to live in such an immediate sense of my presence that every time you sit down to eat, you know I am with you, giving myself to you, providing for your every need.

Every time you drink in fellowship with others, remember that Jesus' blood cleansed and redeemed you, making you acceptable in my sight. **I don't want this to be a piece of religious ritual, but a sharing of my life and the redeeming love made possible through the sacrifice of my Son.**

The first believers met and broke bread together every day. They lived in the immediate sense of Jesus' risen presence. How I wish my people would return to what I intended! I want my holy presence to sanctify their homes as much as when they come together in corporate worship.

Dear child, **live in the immediate sense of my presence.** Whenever you break bread, I am giving myself to you; not just to nourish your physical body, but to feed you spiritually. Every time you bless the cup, you drink the saving grace and mercy of your God.

John 6:50–8; Luke 22:19–20; Acts 2:42,46.

98

Jesus Is Your Righteousness

———— o ————

**"It is because of him that you are in Christ Jesus, who
has become for us wisdom from God."**

(1 Cor. 1:30)

My dear child, I have placed you in Christ Jesus. I
did this when you put your faith in him. **Now his
life is your life, his inheritance your inheritance. You
are a co-heir with him!**

Jesus is your wisdom, the wisdom I provided to bring
you to myself. He has done for you what you could
never do for yourself. He has already achieved what
you could never achieve, no matter how hard you try
to please me. "For in the gospel a righteousness from
God is revealed; a righteousness that is by faith from
first to last."

Jesus is your righteousness. It is pointless, therefore,
to try and achieve a righteousness of your own.

Those who try to do this may call themselves Christians and go to church. They may think of themselves
as good people and aim at behaving in a morally correct
manner, but if they imagine I will accept them on the
basis of their own efforts they will be sadly disappointed. They have no true concept of righteousness.
They fail to realise that their sin and unbelief disqualify
them. They need a Saviour to be their righteousness.

Their righteousness must exceed that of the Scribes and Pharisees!

People don't enter my Kingdom through effort. It is my gift to those who turn to me. You cannot earn righteousness; **I make you righteous through faith.**

"This righteousness from God comes through faith in Jesus Christ to all who believe."

No matter how much you tried, you could never make your own way to heaven. You could not make yourself eternal. You could never deserve the gift of my life. **So I have made you righteous and acceptable in my sight through Jesus.** He offered his righteous life to me on the cross on your behalf, and for everyone in every generation who has sinned.

You are already made acceptable in my sight through him. You don't have to earn my acceptance. It is better to know you have righteousness than to try and achieve it.

Rejoice in the righteousness I have given you. Jesus' life is your life because of your faith in him.

Beloved child, don't think of yourself as unrighteous. Don't imagine your past sin and failure continues to separate you from me. Rejoice that you belong to my Kingdom, that there is no condemnation for those who belong to Christ Jesus.

Pray and work for others to be saved. Your joy will be a witness to those who need to see from your life that my Kingdom is righteousness, peace and joy in the Holy Spirit.

Rom. 5:1–2; 2 Cor. 4:4; 1 Cor. 2:6–8; Rom. 3:9–28.

99

Jesus Is Your Holiness

——— ∘ ———

"Without holiness no-one will see the Lord."
(Heb. 12:14)

My beloved child, there is no need to be afraid of holiness; I already see you as holy! Does this surprise you? You look at yourself, some of your thoughts and actions, and wonder how I, the Holy One, could possibly regard you as holy!

Well, you must never lose sight of what I have done for you through Jesus. I have placed you in him. I don't look at you apart from him, therefore. Your place before me is assured because you are in him.

Because he is righteous, I regard you as righteous. Because he is holy, I see you as holy in him.

Now I want you to live according to this position I have given you. Because you are righteous and holy according to your new nature, I want you to live in righteousness and holiness.

You will never succeed in doing this by looking back on what you were. I have forgiven all your past unrighteousness and unholiness. So why consider these things as if they are still an influence on your life? They cannot affect you now because they no longer exist.

Your problem lies in your thinking, child. You don't think of yourself as holy and righteous; so you don't expect to live in holiness and righteousness. You anticipate failure, not success.

That is unbelief concerning what I have done for you through Jesus. Do you not see that your thinking needs to be renewed so that all your attitudes come in line with my word?

Beloved, because you are light, you don't have to walk in darkness. Of course you can still choose to do so. If you want to be unholy and unrighteous you have the freedom to make that choice. However, if you do you go against your new nature – Christ in you.

This is the crux of the matter, beloved. You have tried to do what is right, feeling all the time that you are fighting against your sinful nature. But the old nature was crucified with Christ. The water of baptism signified that this old life was dead and buried. **Your true nature now is the new nature I have given you: Christ in you. You have a new heart and I have put a new Spirit within you.**

Think of yourself, therefore, as a saint not a sinner. You are sanctified, set apart for me and my purposes. Today you can live a holy and righteous life; you can do what pleases me!

Will you act perfectly? No, I realise that. But it is time for you to know once and for all that your position before me does not depend on what you have done, but on what Jesus has done for you.

You are like a child that is growing and developing. As your Father I love you, accept you and enjoy you at each stage of your development. I will continue to teach, train and refine you to bring you to spiritual maturity and fruitfulness. Increasingly you will reflect your new nature and realise that your past has no hold over you.

Beloved child, I see you as righteous in your new nature – and growing in righteousness. I see you as holy – and growing in holiness.

So be encouraged. I have everything in hand, including you! I will bring you to the fulfilment of the plans I have for you.

1 Cor. 1:30; Rom. 12:2; Gal. 2:20; 1 Cor. 6:11.

100

You Are Holy

———— ○ ————

"But now he has reconciled you by Christ's physical body through death to present you holy in his sight, without blemish and free from accusation."

(Col. 1:22)

I am holy, Jesus is holy and my Spirit is holy. Because you are one with me and my Son, you also are holy. **Jesus is your holiness.** My Holy Spirit lives in you so that his holiness may be expressed in your life.

Dear child, I repeat these truths to you over and over again because you need to hear them continually. You have been so conditioned by thinking negatively about yourself, I am now having to teach you to think the truth! Holiness is not an impossibility for you. And it is not being pious, either!

To be holy is to be whole, complete, perfect. Because you live in him, I see you already seated with me in heavenly places, that work of perfection completed! **I see you already made holy, complete and perfect.** Isn't that wonderful? You did nothing to achieve this. You simply put your faith in Jesus and all he had done for you.

Holiness is a reality for any who put their faith in Jesus. Even you! **You are holy.** That is your position before me. To be holy is to be set apart for my purposes. I want to see the practical outworking of this holiness in your life. You are holy and are called to be holy. Therefore, you are to live in the holiness you have been given, as one set apart for me and my Kingdom.

Without holiness no one will see me face to face. Because you are made holy you need not fear being rejected, judged and found wanting. Rather, rejoice! All heaven rejoiced over you when you turned to me in repentance. I rejoice over you with singing because you belong to me.

Now clearly this is to have practical implications in the way you live each day. Jesus lived a holy life while on earth. To live in holiness is to live like Jesus, therefore. Love is an aspect of my holy life; so is joy, and peace, and patience and all the other fruit of my Holy Spirit.

In holiness Jesus healed the sick and delivered those in bondage. He reached out to others with the truth. He was humble, gentle, authoritative and righteous in all his ways.

All these are aspects of holiness. To be holy is to live in the fullness of life that Jesus came to give you, child.

I have given you my Spirit to empower you to do all that I ask of you. Don't try to live a holy life in your own strength. **Jesus' holy life and nature can shine through your life, weak though you are in yourself.**

You still have the ability to please or displease me by the way you think and behave. Your loving obedience pleases me and enables you to be a blessing to others.

Do you want to be holy? Do you want to be like Jesus? Live in the fullness of his love and power. Don't compromise with the things of the flesh. To live to please yourself is a denial of holiness, of being set apart for me and my purposes. But if you deny yourself, take up your cross and follow Jesus; his holiness will be expressed in you.

And be encouraged by this: you are much holier than you used to be. I can see the improvement!

Heb. 10:10; 1 Pet. 1:15; 2 Cor. 7:1.

101

I Have Redeemed You

———— o ————

"Jesus Christ, who gave himself for us to redeem us from all wickedness and to purify for himself a people that are his very own."

(Titus 2:13–14)

I came in my Son to redeem my people, to purchase them for myself. The cross overshadowed his life from the beginning. It would not be enough to teach the truth, heal the sick or even raise the dead. He would have to be the One who died as a substitute for all those who have sinned.

I had to produce a way to save my people from the wrath and judgment they deserved because of their sin and rebellion against me. Jesus is that Way. I have saved you from your sins, your enemies and from the hands of all who hate you because you have put your faith in him.

I have rescued you from the fate that you deserved and I enable you to serve me without fear. You can walk in holiness and righteousness all the days of your life – because of him! You can experience my mercy continually. So you need not fear failure. Rather, you can rejoice in my grace. You have chosen Jesus because I have chosen you. Yes, beloved, I wanted you for myself, to be my own child by adoption.

Beloved, I have redeemed you. I paid the price for you with Jesus' blood so that you could belong to me. Every debt you could ever owe me has been paid. Every punishment you deserve for your sin, disobedience and rebellion has been paid. It is great to know you are free of debt, isn't it?

The only debt you have now is the debt of love: to love me with all your heart, mind, soul and strength.

Even as I carefully chose Mary to bear my Son, so I have carefully chosen you to bear him in your heart, for your body to be a temple of his Spirit.

Do you recognise the privilege that is yours, beloved child? I have opened your blind eyes that you might see the truth. I have opened your ears that you may hear and understand. So rejoice in me, beloved.

Like Mary, treasure my words in your heart. Ponder them and live in the good of them.

Titus 2:14; Eph. 1:4–5; 1 Cor. 6:19.

102

Eternal Destinies

—— o ——

"Whoever believes in the Son has eternal life, but whoever rejects the Son will not see life, for God's wrath remains on him."

(John 3:36)

When Jesus returns he will send angels to gather the wicked who have opposed me. Until then, the unrighteous are left to grow among those who belong to my Kingdom.

The farmer does not try to pull up the weeds in his field in case he damages the crop. **The righteous and unrighteous must both grow up together until my angels come to harvest.** Then those who belong to the evil one will be thrown into the fire of judgment; but those who are my righteous children will be raised to eternal life. They will reign with me in the glory of my Kingdom for ever.

These things will surely come to pass. Don't listen to those who say that everyone will go to heaven. Don't listen to those who say that God would not reject anyone. All who sin deserve to be rejected and condemned. By my love I have made salvation possible. Those who come to the cross of Jesus to be cleansed of their sins are made worthy in my sight. They are accepted, not rejected; forgiven, not condemned.

Those who don't believe are condemned already because of their unbelief. It is not my desire to condemn them. They have made their choice and rejected me. **To reject me as Lord and Saviour is to reject heaven.**

Dear child, use every opportunity to make my Kingdom known to others. Reveal the truth of my gospel to those who are living in foolishness and deception. Reveal my love to them. Let your light shine in the darkness of the world around you. And rejoice over every soul that is saved, snatched from the grip of Satan and brought into lasting fellowship with me.

Matt. 13:24–30; John 3:16–18; Matt. 5:14–16.

103

Love, Give, Serve

——— ○ ———

"Love one another. As I have loved you, so you must love one another."

(John 13:34)

In the parable of the Good Samaritan the religious ones passed by on the other side, refusing to help the man who had been attacked. They were more concerned with keeping their ritual purity than showing love and compassion to one in need. I prefer mercy to sacrifice. Go and discover what that means.

You will need to be merciful again and again. It is not a question of loving those who deserve to be loved, but those who need to be loved. I want you to have a merciful and loving heart, so that you respond in the right way to situations as they arise.

Sometimes you will be able to share my gospel with those who have corrupt lives; they have used other people, abused their privileges and seem most undeserving. But if I have worked in their hearts to create in them a desire to know me, who are you to judge them? Don't judge; show them my love. **Reveal to them the joys of my Kingdom, so that they long to know me and become part of my family.**

Don't be content to meet material needs without offering others the keys to eternal life. What does it profit them if they have enough to eat, but lack the life of my Kingdom?

Beloved, faith without works is dead. **Genuine faith produces the works of faith – faith that is expressed through love.** And my love is expressed in giving. You demonstrate the presence of my Kingdom through love. Dear child, compassion and concern are not enough; bind up the wounds of the needy. Whatever you do to the least of these, you do to me!

Luke 10:25–37; Jas. 2:20–4, 26; 1 John 3:18; Gal. 5:6.

104

Teach Us To Pray

———— o ————

"The prayer of a righteous man is powerful and effective."

(Jas. 5:16)

When they asked Jesus to teach them to pray, he gave his disciples "The Lord's Prayer". This was not meant to become a formula of words to be mindlessly repeated or chanted. It is prayer about my sovereign reign and directs you to the key subjects to be covered when you pray.

Call me "Father" because you are my child, and you approach me in the bond of love which unites us. I am your Father in heaven, where I reign in victory, glory and power. You are not praying to a weak human father, whose power is restricted. **You are praying to your heavenly Father whose love for you is unlimited and whose power knows no bounds.**

I am holy; therefore my name is to be hallowed. I am to be praised because I alone am worthy of worship.

I want my Kingdom to come and my will to be done on earth as it is in heaven. Recognise that I want on earth what is already established in heaven. There is no sin or sickness in heaven; so Jesus waged war on both!

When you pray that my will is done on earth as in heaven, you pray that everything that curses mankind will be removed; **that my Kingdom of love, power, righteousness and peace will be extended.** To pray this meaningfully means that you make yourself available to be part of the answer to your own prayer.

Ask me to supply your daily bread. **It is my will to give you everything you need to live as a child of my Kingdom.** I give to you for your own good, and as a testimony to others of my generosity to those who trust me.

I am ready to forgive you for the ways in which you do not demonstrate the life of my Kingdom. But you are to forgive those who have sinned against you. If you forgive them, I forgive you; but if you refuse to forgive, you are left in your sins.

Pray that you will not be led into temptation but you will walk in the way of righteousness, for my Kingdom is righteousness, peace and joy in the Holy Spirit. Beloved, I will keep you from the evil one, who seeks to oppose the work of my Kingdom. **Be full of praise that the Kingdom, the power and the glory belong to me; and be thankful that they are your inheritance.**

Matt. 6:9–13; Rom. 8:14–16; Rev. 4:8; Isa. 53:5; Phil. 4:19; 1 John 5:18.

105

Believe You Have Received

———— o ————

"Cast all your anxiety on him because he cares for you."

(1 Pet. 5:7)

D ear child, sometimes I want to give to you but you are not prepared to receive from me. There can be several reasons for this. You don't give yourself time to be still in my presence. You rush around in your own activity, and this makes it impossible to receive what I want to give.

You don't believe I really want to give to you because you consider yourself unworthy to receive.

Sometimes you listen to those who suggest you must bear your problems yourself. They tell you to accept them as my will for you, despite the fact that Jesus carried all your burdens to the cross to free you from them.

Cast all your burdens on me; this is both an invitation and a command. Humble yourself before me, acknowledge your need and then trust me to meet it.

Jesus teaches that whatever you ask for in prayer you will receive, if you believe. **When you pray with faith you believe you have received before there is any external evidence to substantiate such confidence.** You realise there is nothing to be concerned or anxious about; the matter is in my hands.

There is no point in pretending you believe like that when you don't. You cannot make yourself believe you have already received. Better to be honest with me and with yourself. Acknowledge your lack of faith, receive my forgiveness and ask me to speak a word of faith to your heart. I love to answer such prayers.

When you believe you have received, your heart is full of thanksgiving. You know in your heart that your prayer is answered before there is any outward manifestation of healing or change in your circumstances. **At other times you simply accept the authority of the word I speak to you.**

The ten lepers were not healed instantly by Jesus. He told them to go to the priests whose responsibility it was to verify healings. As they went on their way in obedience to the command given them by Jesus, they were healed. They acted on his word.

Healing, or the answer to any other need, doesn't always happen instantaneously, does it, child? You can't dictate to me how you want to be healed or the way I am to answer you. Simply believe the word I speak to you and you will indeed receive from me.

Ps. 130:5; Isa. 53:4–6; 1 Pet. 5:6–7; John 14:13–14; Luke 17:11–14.

106

Persevere In Asking

———— ◦ ————

"If you, then, though you are evil, know how to give good gifts to your children, how much more will your Father in heaven give good gifts to those who ask him!"
(Matt. 7:11)

If you trust me you will have no worries, even about what to wear or eat! You will not be anxious about tomorrow. Faith is practical in its outworking. Has worry ever helped you? Usually your anxieties have been groundless, haven't they? What a waste of time!

Look around you. Who has made the flowers so beautiful? Who orders the seasons and causes things to grow? Who has created in such fine detail and with such wonderful order? If I can make all this, don't you think I can look after you?

I have promised to do whatever you ask in the name of Jesus. I tell you to ask, seek and knock. Don't give up! **Go on asking until you receive what you need. Determination is a true expression of faith.**

Everyone who continues to seek will find, and to those who persist in knocking, the door of my provision will be opened, whatever the need.

Sometimes you don't expect to receive. You ask, seek and knock without any anticipation that I will answer you. What is the point of praying if you do not expect to be answered?

Every time you pray, believe that you will receive what you ask.

Pray at all times in the Spirit, for he will enable you to pray with faith. You can only pray with genuine faith for whatever is my will, and he will not inspire faith for anything that is opposed to my purpose.

Dear child, there have been occasions when you have given up. You thought it was pointless to go on praying and became resigned to living with the problem. It is very easy to do that, isn't it? But what about my promises? I hold them in abeyance until you return to a position of faith! I am ready to forgive you. Then we can start again. I want to give you the faith you have lacked. Are you ready to receive from me?

Matt. 7:7–11; Jas. 1:6–8; Rom. 8:26–7.

107

I Live In You

———— o ————

**"The mystery that has been kept hidden for ages . . .
Christ in you, the hope of glory."**

(Col. 1:26–7)

My dear child, while Jesus was on earth, I looked forward to his return to heaven. He would be the firstfruit of many I would raise from the dead. And I longed to come and live within my children. Yes, it was good to be present among them; but Jesus died on the cross so I could come and live *in* them by the power of my Spirit. **I longed not only to be with my beloved ones, but to be within them.**

This could not happen until Jesus had returned to heaven in triumph. Then he prayed that his Spirit who had led him victoriously through his manhood, the crucifixion and resurrection, would come to live in all who believed in him.

I live in you. I delight to live in you. This was my choice before it became your desire. "You did not choose me, but I chose you." The victorious Spirit of Jesus lives in you, child.

Why have I chosen you? **Because I am a God of grace.** You have put your faith and confidence in what Jesus did for you on the cross, and so you have reaped the benefit of his death.

I live in you to express my life through you and through the whole Body of Christ on earth.

I need the co-operation of every part of my body to reveal my love to others, to show them that I am full of mercy and grace, slow to anger and abounding in love.

You have a part to play in this purpose, beloved child. Love others as I have loved you. Love them as you love yourself. **Because you are my witness let every aspect of my life be seen in you;** those qualities of joy, peace, patience, kindness, goodness, faithfulness, gentleness and self-control which are the fruit of my Holy Spirit. He is developing these qualities in you.

And remember, beloved, **Jesus promised that you would be filled with power when the Holy Spirit came upon you.** You can do whatever I ask you to do because you have my life and resources within you. By trusting in me you are able to cope with every situation that arises.

John 14:16–18; John 15:16; Col. 3:12–14; Eph. 1:19–20.

108

Be Filled To Overflowing

———— o ————

"Instead, be filled with the Spirit."

(Eph. 5:18)

Dear child, to be baptised in the Holy Spirit is to be submerged in my life by Jesus. This is his personal ministry to you. I have placed the seed of my Kingdom in you and watered it with the living water of the Holy Spirit. I have given you the resources of my Kingdom, and the power to live Kingdom life!

Help those who doubt they have received the Holy Spirit because they haven't had identical experiences to others they know.

Show them that I am faithful to my promise that everyone who asks receives. Even a sinful earthly father wouldn't give a snake to his child who had asked for a fish. Neither would he give him a scorpion instead of an egg, or a stone instead of bread. **As the loving heavenly Father, I know how to give good things to those who ask me.**

Many of my children argue over their theologies of the Holy Spirit; when and how he is received. I am concerned to see the reality of my Spirit's life expressed in their lives. It is not the theory that concerns me, but the evidence in believers of his life, of his love and of his power.

I don't contrast the fruit and the gifts of my Spirit; I want to see both expressed together in the lives of all my children. If you ask for a gift that you need I make that gift available to you. And I am constantly at work within you causing the fruit to grow and develop.

My Spirit will cause rivers of living water to flow out of your innermost being. You cannot possibly hide all I put into you. My life will overflow, touching the lives of others around you.

Beloved child, never hesitate to ask for my Spirit to be released afresh in you. **Go on being filled with my Spirit.**

Luke 11:9–13; 1 Cor. 1:7; John 7:37–9.

109

You Live In Me

———— ° ————

"We know that we live in him and he in us, because he has given us of his Spirit."

(1 John 4:13)

J esus is the true Vine. Beloved, **you are a branch living in him.** You cannot exist apart from the Vine. You are a living part of Jesus.

The sap of my Spirit flows through every branch. My life flows through your life to enable you to grow spiritually and produce fruit. I have given you natural abilities; but I am pleased when you trust in my supernatural power. Through my Spirit working in you, lasting fruit is produced. Others are able to receive my life and love because of you.

I have done much pruning and refining in you, cutting out the things which are fruitless and unprofitable. This has proved painful at times, but it has been worthwhile, hasn't it, child? For the things of the flesh war against the things of my Spirit. **And I am teaching you to walk in my Spirit; then you will not gratify the desires of the flesh, those selfish desires which are opposed to my purpose for you.**

Jesus and I have come to make our home with you. I am teaching you to live in close fellowship with me, depending on me in all things, knowing that all my resources are available to you. I fill you with love, so that you can love others with my love. When you need wisdom, power, healing or direction, I am ready to give them to you.

Like the first apostles, I want you to learn that apart from me you can do nothing. Anything you do outside of me is worthless. It makes no sense for me to live in you and you to live in me, yet ignore my presence, or behave as if I was not present.

Because you live in me and I in you, I can reproduce my character in you. Instead of being impatient and intolerant, criticising and judging others, you can express my tender mercy and compassion towards them. Instead of being motivated by self-interest, you can be generous in the way you give yourself to others. You can decide to live for them and not for yourself, realising that in doing so you live for me.

It is much better to abide in my love than try to achieve those things by your own self-effort. Beloved, you are my ambassador, my witness. Yes, I am confident that more and more of my character can be expressed through your life; that is why I have come to live in you. You will not disappoint me!

John 15:1–8; Gal. 5:16–17; John 14:23; Phil. 2:3–4.

110

Your Heart Attitude

———— o ————

"Search me, O God, and know my heart . . . See if there is any offensive way in me."

(Ps. 139:23–4)

A tree is known by its fruit. A good tree produces good fruit because the heart of the tree is good. Another tree may appear good; but if you see that its fruit is bad, you know something is wrong with the heart of the tree, even though the disease may be invisible to the eye.

In the same way you can determine what is in the heart of others by the fruit they bear. The one who has a new heart will bear the fruit of the Spirit in his life. The one who has come to a place of true repentance will bear the fruit of repentance. The one who lives by faith will manifest the fruit of faith. The one who trusts me for the supernatural, miraculous working of my power in his life will see the miracles.

The one who believes the truth of my word in his heart will speak that truth. From the overflow of his heart, his mouth will speak.

You have been perplexed about difficult circumstances I have allowed in your life. Every one of these circumstances has in some way revealed what is in your heart by the way you have reacted to them. When you grumble and complain about your situation, you reveal your heart attitude. If you rejoice despite the circumstances, you demonstrate that your heart is full of faith in me and my words of promise. I have to show you what is in your heart; then you can ask me to purify those things which are a contradiction to my purpose.

Faith without works is dead. Those with dead faith believe certain propositions about me, but don't trust me in their daily circumstances. They don't produce the works of faith. People can believe in my love without loving others. Such faith is dead. You may reach out to others in love, or you may avoid the cost of doing so, demonstrating the limitations of love in your heart.

The one with a living faith loves others because I love him or her. He or she will produce the works of faith. You cannot bear the right fruit without the right heart. This is why I keep a check on your heart, and show you things about yourself you need to see, uncomfortable though they may be at times.

Because you want to live by faith, you will produce the works of faith; things which cannot be accomplished through purely human resources of love and compassion. I know you often feel inadequate. Don't you see, beloved, that is a good reason to trust me and to ask for my Spirit to come to your help! He will! He lives in you to help you in every situation every day of your life. Please don't waste his presence.

Ps. 139:23–4; Luke 6:43–5; Jas. 2:14–24.

111

My Word In You

———— o ————

"Everything is possible for him who believes."
(Mark 9:23)

My beloved, true spirituality is very practical. You don't live in me so that you can wander around in some kind of spiritual daze. Jesus was a man of prayer but his ministry was intensely practical. Life for him was not continuous prayer meetings. He expressed his prayer of faith in a life of faith. He served people, taught them, cared for them and healed them.

Every day of your life, I live in you and you live in me so that things can happen! The supernatural life of my Spirit can break into the practical circumstances of your life. And you can use my powerful resources to touch others' lives.

You can try to find your own natural solution to difficulties, or you can pray with faith, expecting to see my supernatural power at work. Which would you prefer?

When Jesus told his disciples to feed five thousand people, they looked at the situation from a natural standpoint. There was nowhere to buy food in such a remote place, and they didn't have sufficient funds to provide for so many.

Jesus looked at the situation supernaturally, with the eyes of faith. He prayed and acted in faith. Five loaves and two small fish fed all those people with an abundance remaining. Men try to rationalise such incidents, but it is impossible to contain the supernatural working of my Spirit within the reason.

You are learning to live each day in faith. There are still times when you rely on your natural abilities instead of my power, aren't there, child? I don't despair when you fail. **You will learn that every time you trust in yourself things seem difficult; when you trust in me, mountains of need are moved.** I am patient with you while you learn.

Just as Jesus could do nothing by himself to accomplish my purposes, neither can you! As I worked with him so I will work with you.

I showed Jesus what I wanted him to do. I will do the same with you. There is no point trying to take the initiative away from me; you will only end up doing the wrong things if you do.

Many of my children are impatient. They don't wait for me to show them what I want them to do. They rush around in a blaze of fleshly activity and then wonder why there is so little fruit. When they do what I want, the outcome is always profitable both for them and for my Kingdom.

So, beloved, I want you to have my supernatural perspective on the situations you encounter. As you pray, listen to the voice of my Spirit. Let him show you how to pray and tell you what you must do. You are able to hear his voice for he lives in you. Those who are led by my Spirit are my sons! And you know beyond doubt that you are my child!

Matt. 14:13–21; Matt. 17:20; John 15:5.

112

A Servant Heart

———— o ————

"Therefore, whoever humbles himself like this child is the greatest in the kingdom of heaven."

(Matt. 18:4)

After the Transfiguration, Jesus journeyed to Capernaum with his disciples. He could overhear their conversation. When they arrived at their destination he asked what they were discussing on the way. They were embarrassed by his question and at first no one wanted to answer.

They were questioning who among them was greatest! Beware of the temptation of thinking that the experiences you have in prayer make you more important than others. Do you see why he instructed them not to tell anyone what had happened on the mountain until he had ascended to glory? Nevertheless, it was tempting to think they were better than the others because of the great privilege granted to them.

Jesus made it clear that **the greatest in my eyes are the servants of all, those who have a sober estimate of themselves, regardless of the experiences they have, the privileges accorded them, or the great ways in which I use them.**

Imagine walking along with the Son of God and arguing about who is greatest! The principles of my heavenly

Kingdom are very different from the principles of this world. Worldly people consider the greatest to be those who have most material possessions or natural abilities, those who are famous and envied by others.

The greatest in my Kingdom are those who lovingly, obediently and faithfully serve me by loving and serving others. They don't look for praise; they don't want fame. They are not interested in a worldly reward for their work. To know they serve the King of kings is reward enough.

Jesus came as the One who served. He washed the disciples' feet and made it clear they could not be one with him unless they allowed him to serve them. They had to learn that **servants also need to be served!**

Some of my children want to serve others but they don't allow me to serve them, neither are they good at allowing others to serve them. **A true servant will be humble enough to receive from others, as well as give to them.**

Remain humble before God and man, my child. Let me serve you by cleansing you and giving to you. Then go in my name to love and serve others in the same way I love and serve you. Even though I use you in ways that are a blessing to others, keep a servant heart, rejoicing to live for others and not for yourself. Your reward will be great in heaven.

Mark 9:33–7; John 13:6–17; Phil. 2:3–8; Jas. 4:10.

113

Follow Me

———— o ————

"Anyone who does not take his cross and follow me is not worthy of me."

(Matt. 10:38)

I f you seek to save your life you will lose it; but if you lose your life for the sake of the gospel you will find it. Those who try to hold on to their lives, their time, ambitions or money for themselves, deny my Lordship over every area of their lives. Your soul is eternal, but not your possessions.

Beloved, if my Kingdom is first in your life you appreciate that you only live for me by living for others. Your love for me is expressed in the way you live for the other members of my family. **Your love for me is shown to be genuine by the way you love others.** Don't concentrate on others' inadequacies and failures. Instead of criticising them, pray for them and encourage them.

I don't criticise you; I encourage you to walk in my ways.

I want all my children to love and accept one another. I want them to demonstrate to the world a love and unity that cannot be found anywhere except within my family.

The work of my Kingdom is so vital there is no time for my children to squabble amongst themselves. I want them to respect and honour one another; to unite in my purpose of making me known to others. I have given my Holy Spirit to create such unity in my Church.

Don't worry about the cost of following me or what the future will hold for you. I give you this assurance: if you give your life to me for the sake of my Kingdom as the priority in your life, laying down your life for your brothers by living for them and not yourself, then everything you need will be added to you. You will not have to worry about what to eat or wear. **You will not need to be anxious about the future, but can trust my promises to provide for you.**

Beloved, I am faithful and will keep every word of promise I have given you.

I will never leave you or forsake you. I will guard you and keep you as the apple of my eye!

Matt. 10:38–9; 1 John 3:16–18; 1 John 4:19–21; Matt. 6:25,33.

114

Speak of My Goodness

———— o ————

"I have . . . plans to prosper you and not to harm you, plans to give you hope and a future."

(Jer. 29:11)

D o not fall into a negative way of thinking, expecting life will be full of difficulties and the way ahead continually hard. I have prepared good things for you to enjoy. You follow the *Good* Shepherd who leads you beside still waters and into rich pastures. I cause your cup to overflow and spread a table of blessing before you in the face of your enemies.

Jesus has triumphed over everything that could oppose you. He made a public spectacle of all the powers of darkness, overcoming them by the blood of the cross. **The way you overcome is through the power of that blood and by the word of your testimony.** This is why it is important to speak in faith, declaring what I have done for you through my Son. When you share your faith, clouds of heaviness lift and joy fills your heart. Speaking to others about me strengthens your own faith.

If you want to be in line with my will, your tongue must agree with my word and not contradict what I say. **Speak of yourself as one who is greatly blessed, highly esteemed by your God, precious in his sight, honoured, accepted, loved, wanted and appreciated.**

Don't let the enemy deceive you into thinking otherwise.

Don't expect the worst, or that is what you will receive. My purpose for you is good. I have given you life in all its fullness. I have prepared good things for you to walk in.

You are a child of faith. I give you faith to cope with every situation. Listen to what I say; then do it. **If your thinking is in line with my word, then your speaking will be full of faith.** Your expectations will be positive and you will stop contradicting what I say about you. From the overflow of your heart, your mouth will speak faith. You will expect victory, not defeat; provision, not lack; health, not sickness. I am teaching you to expect the very best!

Beloved, you can tell where others are in their faith simply by listening to them in conversation. They can also determine where you are by listening to you! And I always know what you believe because I can read your heart! You give me joy whenever I see that you trust me!

Ps. 23; Col. 2:15; Rev. 12:11; John 10:10; Luke 6:43–5.

115

Rejoice Always

———— o ————

"Rejoice in the Lord always. I will say it again: Rejoice!"

(Phil. 4:4)

D ear child, you cannot rejoice and grumble at the same time. Grumbling suggests I have lost control of the situation, that I don't really care, or am unaware of your problem. A grumbling heart is not a believing heart. Complaining never achieves anything. It only makes matters worse and makes others miserable.

I know you wonder sometimes why I have allowed difficulties in your life. You question why I have not taken steps to prevent the more traumatic events. I haven't promised you an easy life but a victorious one! Victory assumes that there are things which need to be overcome.

The testing you experience proves your faith is genuine. **You are a great witness when you maintain your trust in me in the midst of all the difficulties you encounter.**

I don't want you to grumble when there is an attack from the enemy; use your spiritual authority to resist him and then you will see him flee from you.

I don't want you to complain when you have to go through trials and temptation. I am at hand to help you and will not allow you to be tempted beyond your ability to resist. You can say "No" to temptation.

I don't want you to be resentful about the opposition and hurt you encounter. You have the ability to forgive those who wrong you and the faith to overcome every difficulty. Why be resentful?

I will carry you through any and every situation. Paul discovered the secret of being content in every situation. Consider what he suffered for the sake of the gospel!

This doesn't mean you are to be content to live with the problems that arise. No, far from it. **The testing of your faith is not a matter of enduring the problem but of overcoming it, of seeing the mountain moved.**

Beloved, I promise to meet every need of yours according to my glorious riches made available to you in Christ. You are a co-heir with Christ. Why complain? When you feel like grumbling, this is the very time to give thanks and rejoice in me. Take your eyes off your feelings and problems and place them on the truth of my word. Come into my presence with thanksgiving, and you will soon see things in a different light!

You will realise that I am still in control!

Phil. 2:14–16; 1 Cor. 15:57; 1 Pet. 1:6–7; 1 Cor. 10:13; Phil. 4:19.

116

Pray at all Times with Thanksgiving

———— o ————

"Give thanks in all circumstances, for this is God's will
for you in Christ Jesus."

(1 Thess. 5:18)

It is easy to thank me when everything seems to be
going well; much more difficult when you are confronted with problems. When you entrust a situation to
me without seeing any visible change immediately, you
find it hard to thank me for having the matter in hand;
you like to see some evidence to indicate I am doing
something about your dilemma.

Dear child, thanking me is evidence that you trust me
to change the situation and overcome the problems even
before you see any visible change. You are not truly in a
position of faith until you do thank me from your heart. **The
prayer of faith is always accompanied with thanksgiving.**
How can you believe you have received, without being
thankful? Faith is being sure of what you do not see.

You are thankful when someone gives you a gift, or
even the promise of a gift – provided you believe he will
be faithful to the promise. If you are not thankful this
indicates that you don't believe it is the person's intention to give to you.

It is the same when you pray. If you believe it is my
intention to give to you, you will automatically thank

me, even though there may be no visible or immediate evidence of the answer. The promise of the gift is sufficient. You live in the good of that promise. Can you see why I tell you to pray at all times with thanksgiving?

I know your need before you ask, beloved. I hear you when you pray. If you are confident of this, then you can be sure you receive whatever you ask in my name.

You see, child, I want you to have a thankful heart so that your spontaneous reaction to difficulty is one of faith. You inevitably rejoice that I am with you and you trust me to resolve the situation. You are so confident in my love that you know that is what I want to do!

Phil. 4:6; Heb. 11:1; 1 John 5:14–15; Matt. 6:7–8.

117

Keep Rejoicing

—— ○ ——

"Be joyful always; pray continually; give thanks in all circumstances, for this is God's will for you in Christ Jesus."

(1 Thess. 5:16–18)

Joy and thanksgiving go together. Rejoicing is not putting a brave face on things to disguise a mournful heart. It is not smiling outwardly while inwardly you are feeling angry or full of self-pity. The joy has to come from your heart. **When you believe what I promise, you have every cause to rejoice and be glad, even though your situation may seem desperate.**

You rejoice when I answer your prayers, when I bless you or heal you. You rejoice that I have done specific things in your life, such as filling you with my Holy Spirit. But sometimes you have resented the circumstances I have allowed in your life. Your reaction has been one of anger or anxiety rather than joy or faith.

I want you to rejoice **always**. Give thanks in **all** circumstances. Agree with me that you will do this, and you will see remarkable changes in your life. The decision is yours!

Even when you don't understand what is happening, keep rejoicing because you know I am in charge and I haven't forgotten about you. I am thoroughly faithful and trustworthy in fulfilling every word of promise I have given you.

I am on your side. I love you, I want to encourage and help you.

Keep rejoicing, confident that I am in control, I have heard your prayer and have undertaken to provide for you in whatever way is necessary. **Let the joy of my Spirit in you be expressed, not suppressed, and you will see my power released.**

As long as you resent a situation I do not lift a finger to help you. As soon as you show that you trust me by rejoicing and thanking me, all my resources swing into action!

1 John 5:14; Phil. 4:4–6; 1 Pet. 1:6.

118

Learn From Me

———— ○ ————

"Jesus often withdrew to lonely places and prayed."
(Luke 5:16)

J esus was a man full of joy. He was not the sombre figure many imagine. His joy raised him above his companions and he made it clear that he wanted the disciples to be full of his joy.

This is my purpose for you, beloved. I want you to be full of the joy of Jesus. He enjoyed being with his disciples despite their failure, misunderstanding and lack of faith. He truly loved each one of them. He loved the multitudes he taught, those who came to him in need. He maintained a loving attitude even to those who stubbornly refused to believe the truth.

He enjoyed his ministry; teaching the people and seeing them grow in understanding and wisdom. He enjoyed healing them and seeing them set free from the things which bound them.

As much as he enjoyed people, Jesus made sure he had time to be alone with me. If the day was full of activity, he spent the night alone with me. Nothing was allowed to stand in the way of our times of fellowship.

If you spend time quietly with me, your strength will be renewed. I will encourage you in difficult times, and you will always be refreshed by my presence. You will become more sensitive to the voice of my Spirit. Then you will know my strategy for your life.

If such times of prayer were essential for Jesus, you can be absolutely sure they are essential for you!

The more you enjoy time with me, the more you will enjoy people. If you love me you will love your brothers and sisters also. The time you spend with me will affect your relationships with others and the way I am able to use you to bless them.

Don't think of your times of prayer as a joyless duty. Because I tell you to rejoice in me always, you are to rejoice in your need to draw aside with me in prayer. Yes, beloved, rejoice that I want to have this relationship with you in prayer every day.

Being thankful for all the good things I pour into your life, beloved, will enable you to hear my voice more clearly instead of struggling to know what I am saying. **Yes, rejoicing in me makes you more sensitive to my voice** because praise draws attention away from yourself and causes you to concentrate on me. It doesn't do much good to fill your times of prayer with complaining does it?

Heb. 1:9; John 15:11; Luke 10:21; Luke 6:12; Phil. 4:4–6.

119

Draw Aside With Me

———— o ————

"But when you pray, go into your room, close the door
and pray to your Father, who is unseen."

(Matt. 6:6)

I rejoice in you. Yes, I really do. This is because I love
you. And when you rejoice in me you express your
love for me. Then you can hear my voice of love speaking to your heart.

Reading the scriptures will help you to listen to me.
Receive my word with joy because it is spoken to you
in love.

Store up my words in your heart even though they may
not appear to have particular application at that moment.
At the appropriate time, my Spirit will remind you of the
relevant truths. This is part of his ministry to you.

Learn from the experience and wisdom of others who
walk in close fellowship with me and are anointed
teachers and leaders. But understand that **nothing can
replace the time you spend with me, listening personally to my voice through my word and in prayer.** Some
find it difficult to hear because they spend so little time
listening.

When Jesus chose his twelve disciples, he spent the
previous night in prayer. He knew the importance of

listening to me. He wanted me to guide him in the decisions he made.

Draw aside with me when you have important decisions to make. Don't depend on your own reason. Allow me to guide you.

Those who spend time in prayer are those who become effective in prayer. The only way to learn how to pray is by doing it!

When Jesus drew aside with me, he did so in faith. He was prepared to wait on me until he received the answer. Many of my children give up far too easily. Don't be like that, child. I want you to persevere. I will not withhold the answers you need. I want to guide and direct you.

It is wonderful, isn't it, when you know I have spoken to you? So draw aside and spend time with your heavenly Father. Such occasions are never a waste of time, even when it seems that nothing much has happened. You will not always be aware of my presence, but I am there with you. I work in your spirit rather than in your feelings.

Times spent in prayer and reading my word are a wonderful opportunity to know me better and to hear my voice more clearly.

Come into my presence with joy and you will take that joy into the rest of your life. **If you delight in me you will delight to do my will.** You will delight in what I say to you through my word and by my Spirit.

You can enjoy me with others but nothing can replace those intimate moments when we are alone. The enemy will try to prevent you from spending time with me because he knows the powerful impact that my word and prayer make on your life. Don't listen to his suggestion that such things are a chore or a waste of time. He is threatened when faith is strengthened within you because you hear my voice. And he hates it when you rejoice in me.

Zeph. 3:17; Prov. 2:1–6; Col. 4:2.

120

My Covenant

———— ○ ————

"Christ is the mediator of a new covenant, that those who are called may receive the promised eternal inheritance . . ."

(Heb. 9:15)

A covenant is an agreement between two parties. Under the Old Covenant I promised to bless my people abundantly if they obeyed the commandments I gave them. When they were obedient and faithful I caused them to prosper.

When they grew disobedient or became complacent, turning away from my word, I had to discipline them. If they failed to heed my warnings, I allowed them to be humbled and defeated to bring them back to obedience. Even though I wanted the best for them, I had to discipline them in love.

Beloved, I sent Jesus to inaugurate the New Covenant of which you are a part. The promises of the Old Covenant are good; but the life and promises of the New are even better. Those who believe in him inherit all the blessings I have promised under either covenant.

I didn't need to make a covenant with my people; I chose to do so. Because I am faithful, I am not afraid to bind myself to keep my word. **I will never change my word or dishonour the agreement I have made with**

those who put their faith in me. Even if men prove faithless, I will always remain faithful. I will do what I have said I will do.

You are mine, a child of my covenant. You have decided to give your life to me, and I have given my life to you. I want you to have my best. Walk in my ways, believe my promises and you will see my word fulfilled in your life. If you abide in me and my words abide in you, then you can ask me for whatever you wish and it will be given you.

Dear child, I am not a man that I should lie. I watch over the words I have spoken to ensure they are fulfilled. I will not fail to keep any of my promises to you or to any of my children.

2 Cor. 1:20; Heb. 8:7–13; John 15:7; 1 Sam. 15:29.

121

I Am Faithful to My Word

———— o ————

"He who is the Glory of Israel does not lie or change his mind; for he is not a man, that he should change his mind."

(1 Sam. 15:29)

I love faithfulness because I myself am faithful. Jesus is the mediator of the New Covenant I have established with my children and the guarantor that every promise given under that covenant will be fulfilled. Every word I have spoken will come to pass.

Because you are a child of the New Covenant, all my promises belong to you. Jesus is the "Amen", the "So be it", of all those promises. Don't treat them lightly; I have the power to bring about every word I have spoken.

I give you many wonderful promises concerning prayer. Are these idle words? Are they promises to be explained away? Does it seem unrealistic to interpret them literally? What I have said, I have said. I will not revoke a single word.

Whatever you ask me in Jesus' name I will give you.

You will receive whatever you ask in prayer, if you believe.

Whatever you ask in prayer, believe you have received it and it will be yours.

Do you believe my words to you, child? Do you think these are empty promises? No, they are truth! I answer every prayer of faith.

These promises are personally for you, beloved. Take them to heart. Read them often. Declare them boldly whenever you pray. The windows of heaven are open to you. You have access to my throne. Be bold in what you ask, and equally bold in what you expect to happen as a result.

Ps. 33:4,11; 2 Cor. 1:18–20; 2 Pet. 1:3–4; John 14:13–14; Heb. 4:16; Mk 11:24.

122

Stay Close

———— o ————

"For who is he who will devote himself to be close to me?"

(Jer. 30:21)

Beloved, I want you to stay close to me. You have the habit of wandering away. You sometimes draw close and enjoy my presence during times of prayer, but forget I am with you always. I am no further away from you than a prayer; yes, even a quick one! **Every time you look to me with faith, you give opportunity for my supernatural activity.** I can give you my calm assurance and peace in the midst of turmoil, confusion and perplexity. I am ready to undertake for you in every situation.

This is so much better than struggling on your own! Learn to live always in my presence; don't ignore me.

Remember the covenant relationship we have together. I promise that I will never leave you or forsake you because you are mine.

In my love I have been very patient with you, haven't I, child? I know your weakness and every occasion that you fail; but I never push you away from me. Quite the opposite.

I draw you closer to me. I want you close to me. I really do! **I enjoy your company and I want you to enjoy mine!**

Heb. 13:5; Jer. 31:3; Heb. 10:22; Zeph. 3:17.

123

Be Bold

——— o ———

"You may ask me for anything in my name, and I will do it."

(John 14:14)

D ear child, be bold in prayer. Don't give up easily. Ask with confidence and persist in asking until you receive the answer you need.

Jesus told the parable of the persistent widow to teach the disciples to pray without giving up. When people pray formal prayers, this is evidence of the shallowness of their faith, even though they may be sincere. Their failure to pray specifically indicates that they don't believe for specific answers. **What is the point of prayer that does not anticipate a specific result?** I can answer specific requests, but not vague pleasantries!

Before you begin, ask yourself what you believe will happen as a result of your prayer. Then you can pray that answer into being.

How can you believe you have received the answer if you are not sure what you are asking for? A double-minded man is unstable in all his ways and cannot expect to receive anything from me.

Specific prayers receive specific answers! My Spirit will always guide you as to what to pray in every situation. Listen carefully to him.

Beloved, when you know you have heard from me either through scripture or a prophetic word, hold fast to what I say. Don't let go of my word to you. Persist in your believing, regardless of what others say. Don't expect **any** answer, only the **right** one. Don't be content with **any** answer, only the one that meets the need.

Luke 18:1–8; 1 John 5:14–15; Jas. 1:4–8.

124

Freedom from Accusation

———— ○ ————

"If God is for us, who can be against us?"

(Rom. 8:31)

J esus was oppressed more than you will ever be, beloved. All the spiritual powers of darkness were against him. As he hung on the cross, he suffered a sense of total alienation from me. Love is costly! It was difficult enough to see his disciples desert him; to experience separation from me was almost unbearable. This was the ultimate act of love for you and all who have sinned. He suffered that darkness that you might walk in light.

Who can rightly accuse you? No one, not even Satan! You are redeemed, cleansed, forgiven through the innocent blood that was shed on your behalf. That blood is the answer to every accusation, to every attempt by the enemy to make you feel unworthy and condemned. He is defeated, overcome by the blood of Jesus!

Everything has been accomplished for your total salvation, holiness and welfare of spirit, soul and body. There is no need in your life that cannot be met through the power of Jesus' blood.

Those who follow Jesus, the Light of the World, will never walk in darkness; they have the light of life. They can walk in the light as the children of light.

You belong to the light, beloved child. **I have saved and delivered you from all the powers of darkness and they no longer have any claim or hold over you.** You live in the One who is light, in whom there is no darkness at all.

Walk in the light as my child. Live in the truth that will enable you to live in freedom. Don't go back to the darkness. Withstand every temptation of the devil who would love there to be an area of darkness in your soul that he could claim as his territory.

You don't belong to the darkness but to the light. Darkness is anything of which you would be ashamed, should it be brought into the light. I don't want you to live in shame. Aren't you pleased that you have the blood of Jesus to cleanse you and the Holy Spirit to enable you to walk in my ways?

You were once darkness; now you are light in your Lord. The fruit of that light consists in all goodness, righteousness and truth.

Dear beloved child, have nothing to do with the fruitless deeds of darkness. Expose such things to the light; for wherever the light of Jesus shines, sin is exposed and can then be forgiven. The light makes everything visible. Know the cleansing of your Saviour, and the darkness disappears!

1 Pet. 1:18–19; Col. 1:22; Heb. 7:25; John 8:12; Eph. 5:8–14.

125

The Way Of Wisdom

———— o ————

"Small is the gate and narrow the road that leads to life."

(Matt. 7:14)

D ear child, the way of wisdom is narrow. The broad road of foolishness leads to destruction. Many walk on that way. I have taken hold of your life and called you to be my disciple. I lead you on the narrow way, the highway of holiness. No fool may walk there, but only those who belong to me. The lion and wild beasts are not able to touch those who walk on that way; they are kept safe from the devil and his demonic forces. They will enter Zion with singing, and everlasting joy shall be on their lips.

The right way is narrow, but it is the way of victory, liberty and joy. Righteousness brings more joy and greater satisfaction than indulging your fleshly instincts. **And I have made you righteous so that you can walk in right ways!** Righteousness and wickedness have nothing in common. To walk on the narrow way is an expression of your love for me. There are great rewards for righteousness. Obedience brings peace and a constant revelation of my love.

The one who hears and *puts my word into practice* is the wise man who builds on a rock. The one who hears what I say but fails to do it is like the foolish man who builds on sand. His house falls when the storms of life rage against him, while the wise man's house stands firm.

Beloved, ensure that all four "walls" of your life are on rock. If one wall is on sand there will be subsidence and the house will be seriously weakened and could fall!

Matt. 7:13–14; Isa. 35:8–10; Matt. 7:24–7.

126

Keep Yourself Pure

———— ° ————

"Whatever is pure, whatever is lovely . . . think about such things."

(Phil. 4:8)

Beloved child, set your mind on whatever is pure and lovely. If you think about what is impure you will want that. Sin is first conceived in the mind. This is why you need to take your thoughts captive and bring them in line with the truth. You are to control your thoughts, not allow them to control you.

Don't be drawn into the sin of others around you. Because others are negative and critical, this doesn't mean that you are to be like them. Stand against all deceit and corruption. Don't be a party to such things, even if it is costly to expose them. It is better to please me than to please others by joining them in their sin. So don't yield to peer pressure. You are my witness.

These are your goals: living in righteousness because you live in the Righteous one; living by faith because you live in the truth of my word; living in love, for the only thing that counts is faith expressed in love; living in peace because you are an ambassador for the gospel of peace.

This describes the life I want for you; righteous, faithful, loving and peaceful. Such a life saves you from the corruption of the world around you. And yet such a life is bound to lead you into confrontation with others, as it did with Jesus.

You will compromise the truth if you are afraid of confrontation. My Spirit will give you peace when you need to confront sin. Those who live in darkness and deception are afraid of the truth. If you walk in light and truth you have nothing to fear. And nobody will be able to take your peace from you as you seek to do what is right in each situation.

Understand that, whether you like it or not, you are in the middle of a spiritual battle and you opt out of the fight to your peril. **You are on the side of righteousness against wickedness, deceit and corruption. You are in the Kingdom of light which wages war against the dominion of darkness.**

Beloved, you are my witness in the midst of a society where there is much evil. The devil wants you to be passive, uninvolved and a spectator. I tell you to expose the deeds of darkness. I want your light to shine before men so that they will see your good works and give me glory.

Phil. 4:8–9; 2 Cor. 10:5; Matt. 5:16.

127

Rest Secure

—— ○ ——

"Better the little that the righteous have than the wealth of many wicked; for the power of the wicked will be broken, but the Lord upholds the righteous."

(Ps. 37:16–17)

My dear one, don't envy those who belong to this world, but have rejected my eternal Kingdom. They may seem content with their worldly riches and lifestyle. They may claim to have everything they want. Inwardly, beloved, they are spiritually empty. What of the future? Do they have any hope of heaven?

Because they have no assurance of personal salvation, of my eternal acceptance, they will say that there is no such place as heaven. Alternatively they will claim that I will accept everyone regardless of the way they have lived. They want their "own" gospel; a false gospel. They don't want to face the truth.

If they were to acknowledge that I exist they would know that they should also recognise the claims I have on all who are part of my creation. To believe in heaven as a dwelling place of the Holy One is to say that holiness will be required of those who will be accepted there.

I make it plain that without holiness, no one will see me. Because you have put your faith in Jesus you can rest secure in your salvation. **Therefore, you don't need to envy anyone else. Those who don't belong to my Kingdom should rather envy you for your calm assurance of my love for you.** They have a false confidence, a transitory one. You have the confidence of faith, beloved; faith in One who will never fail you or forsake you.

Live every day in the revelation of that love and you will be a witness to those who don't know me. They will envy your calm assurance for this life and confidence concerning your eternal destiny.

Heb. 12:14; Eph. 1:5–8, 13–14; Prov. 23:17.

128

The Fear of The Lord

———— ∘ ————

"Give me an undivided heart, that I may fear your name."

(Ps. 86:11)

My Spirit of wisdom and understanding rested on Jesus and it rests upon you also because you live in him, beloved child.

To fear me is the beginning of that wisdom. This doesn't mean you are to be scared of me. The more you know my love, the less negative fear will grip you. You will grow in confidence and assurance.

You have access into the Holy of Holies through the blood of Jesus. It is in this most holy of places that you will discover what it is to fear me in the right and proper sense; to be in awe of who I am, to know your own nothingness before the all-Holy God. And yet at the same time to know that I welcome you as a child whom I love and honour.

When the fear of the Lord is upon a person's life, he wants to please me in all things. He dreads stepping out of my will, not because he is afraid of the consequences, but because he does not want to grieve me or offend my love.

Yes, the fear of the Lord is the beginning of wisdom. And I want you to live in wisdom, not foolishness.

Knowing this fear will help you, beloved. **You will desire to keep yourself pure and obedient to my will. You will submit readily to my authority. You will rejoice in those things which cause me to rejoice, and will avoid those things which grieve me.**

Know that the fear of your Lord is pure, enduring for ever. I confide in those who fear me. I store up my goodness for them. My angel encamps around them and I delight in them. I bring them blessing and prosperity.

My child, you want this fear to return to your nation, don't you? For when this is lost to a nation it becomes lawless in its moral and social life. But first the fear needs to be restored to the Church. Without that fear men believe what they want; they disregard my word and are guided by the spirit of error rather than my Spirit of truth.

So pray for the Church and for the nation, child. As you do so, walk in the fear, the awesome and loving respect of your God at all times and in all things.

Ps. 111:10; Ps. 25:14; Ps. 34:7; Ps. 128:1.

129

Faith and Vision

———— o ————

"Who, being in very nature God, did not consider equality with God something to be grasped, but made himself nothing, taking the very nature of a servant." (Phil. 2:6–7)

Jesus, my Son, came as a servant. He demonstrated that the principles of my Kingdom are very different from the principles of this world. Greatness in my Kingdom is not measured by wealth or fame, but by submission to my will, by the willingness to serve.

I promised a servant; yet many of my people didn't recognise him when he came. Even today some look for Jesus in pomp and ceremony, while he lives in the hearts of those who believe my word and obey my commands.

I delighted in the obedience that Jesus showed me, and I always delight in your obedience, beloved child. **My Spirit is upon you as it was upon him to enable you to do what I say.**

The One who came to serve is the One who rules; he proved himself to be the Man of authority. I want you to understand, beloved, that **these qualities are to be seen in you: that you humbly and lovingly serve while faithfully and powerfully exercising the authority I have given you.**

Jesus was concerned for the destiny of the nations. These were his inheritance; the ends of the earth are his possession. Submissively he did all that was necessary for the destiny of the nations to be settled. Those who oppose him shall certainly be pulled down; those who honour him shall be exalted.

I have caused nations who honour my Son to prosper. When they have opposed my word they experience judgment. I laugh at those who laugh at me; and I assure you, child, I shall have the last laugh.

Don't limit your faith to your own personal circumstances or the needs around you. **Stand in opposition to the powers of darkness that want to rule your nation. Don't allow them to have their way.** Remember that I have given you power over all the authority of the evil one. You are one of an army of believers who together are to see your nation liberated from the grip of the enemy.

Does it seem inconsistent to you that I place such a task before you, knowing you feel overawed at the prospect? Consider Jesus. I sent him as the Servant. His submission to my will enabled him to exercise his full authority.

Don't you see that the same principle applies to you? You are both servant and son. You serve me and yet you are a co-heir with Christ. You share in his authority and in his inheritance. **I give to those who believe in me their nation to take as their inheritance. They are to rule and reign in my name, pulling down the strongholds of the enemy, exalting Jesus to his rightful place, enthroned in their hearts and Lord of their nation.**

This is why I want you to be more confident, beloved. I want you to have faith, not only for your own needs, but for the nation around you.

Matt. 23:11; Matt. 28:18–20; 2 Cor. 10:4; Gal. 4:7.

130

Your Nation

————— o —————

"The government will be on his shoulders."

(Isa. 9:6)

D o you believe I can change your nation, not only politically but spiritually? Do you believe I can change the social and moral values of your land? You know I am able, but do you believe I will do these things? Is it not my purpose to bring revival to my Church and a spiritual awakening to the nations? Isn't this why my Son gave his life for you all? Yes, it is my will for all to be saved.

Beloved, who rules your nation? Kings, queens, presidents, governments, politicians, ministers, the councils of men? Have I not placed the government of nations on my Son, on his shoulders?

This is not apparent as you look around you. **But I am raising up a people for myself, those who will be bold and strong in my Spirit. Those who will exercise the spiritual authority I have given them, pulling down the strongholds of the enemy and destroying that which pretentiously sets itself up against Jesus!**

I desire to see the end of oppression. He endured oppression and judgment for the deliverance of my people. It is time for my children to rise up in faith to see my sovereign rule and reign extended.

Have I not said that I will shake the nations? For judgment awaits those who oppose me, but mercy and grace await those who turn to me.

It is true that he who lives in you is greater than he who lives in the world. Very well then, you have nothing to fear from the principalities and powers of darkness. **Exalt Jesus over the affairs of your nation, your area, your immediate district. This land does not belong to the enemy; it is mine.** Understand the spiritual power that is released in heavenly places as you exalt the name of Jesus.

And don't be diffident about sharing my word with others. Be bold and confident. Make the claims of my Lordship clear to them. For all things are to be brought into subjection to the authority of my name and my word.

Beloved, I call you to reign in life!

Isa. 9:2–7; 1 John 5:4; Rom. 8:37; 1 John 4:4; Rom. 5:17.

131

My Triumphal Procession

———— o ————

"But thanks be to God, who always leads us in triumphal procession in Christ."

(2 Cor. 2:14)

Jesus stood silent when falsely accused. Events would justify he was the victim of injustice. For when men had done all they could to him, he emerged victorious from the grave, now to reign in triumph. However, when challenged as to whether he was the Christ, he replied, "I AM!"

I **always** lead you in his triumphal procession. Do you believe this? You don't have to contemplate failure and defeat. Many of my children are guilty of a false humility that is really a form of unbelief. They are silent, not because of meekness, but because of fear.

Like Jesus, you don't have to defend yourself when falsely accused. I will justify my righteous ones. But like Jesus, when challenged about the truth you need to be bold in affirming your faith. **What can men do to you? If I am on your side, who can be against you?** I honour those who honour me before others.

My will prospers in the hands of Jesus. He is working out the destiny of nations. **I set a people of faith in the midst of your nation that their voices might be bold in affirming the truth.** They may seem to be voices in a spiritual wilderness, but I shall ensure their words are heard.

Beloved, nothing can separate you from my love. No trouble, hardship or persecution shall separate you from me. In all these things you are more than a conqueror.

It is not the voice of formal religion that is needed, for this can do nothing to bring salvation to one soul, let alone a nation. No, it is the voice of faith in my word that has to be heard. It is only the knowledge of my Holy One that will bring people to the truth. And you are his witness.

Dear child, your witness is important. Your intercession is significant. Your faith matters. Your victory in spiritual warfare over the enemy is essential. You are part of my plan for your nation.

Ps. 138:3; Prov. 28:1; 2 Cor. 4:13.

132

I Am Coming Soon!

———— o ————

"He who has the Son has life; he who does not have the Son of God does not have life."

(1 John 5:12)

Jesus will come as the Bridegroom to claim his bride. My Church is the bride, but is not yet ready for marriage. Still she has many spots and wrinkles, imperfections and impurities which mar the image of my Son in his Body.

Beloved, in these last days my Spirit will move with refining power to prepare my Church for the Day of my coming. **He will not refine ecclesiastical structures but believers, those who will honour me because of their holy living, their faith in my word and the power that flows from their lives. They are my true witnesses.** In the face of opposition and times of testing they will remain faithful to me.

When Jesus comes, he will gather to himself all who are redeemed through his blood. For them this will be a time of great rejoicing, but for others a time of great catastrophe. The moment when my justice is revealed will be the time of vindication for those whose faith is in me. But those who have sought consolation in their own gods will see the error of their dreadful ways, and will be lost. They will realise they are deserving of my wrath because they have refused to believe in the sacrifice that could save them from that wrath.

It is good that many preach and teach about my love. However, people must be warned about the coming wrath for those who disobey and disbelieve. Remember, I don't want to condemn, but to save. My wrath is tempered by mercy. If they reject my mercy, only wrath remains. Warn others, my beloved. This is your loving responsibility.

Eph. 5:25–7; Matt. 24:30–1, 40–2; Matt. 13:40–3; Rom. 2:5–10.

133

The Future Fulfilment of My Kingdom

———— o ————

"For the Lord himself will come down from heaven, with a loud command . . . And so we will be with the Lord for ever."

(1 Thess. 4:16–17)

What you experience now is only a partial manifestation of my Kingdom. Because of your human weakness you manifest only certain aspects of that Kingdom. Jesus expressed Kingdom life perfectly.

As you look at the world around you, it seems obvious that my sovereign rule is not expressed everywhere. In many ways it looks as if the enemy is in control because he is able to manipulate those who don't believe in me. Yet my rule is established wherever my children live by faith and submit to my Lordship. Every time a person turns to me in faith, I take him out of darkness and place him in the Kingdom of my Son, whom I love.

The final outcome is not in doubt: Jesus will come again in triumph. My Kingdom will be manifested fully on earth. The devil and all his forces will be routed.

Be on the watch for the time of my coming. Be ready and prepared. Don't be like the foolish virgins who were not ready for the coming of the bridegroom. Have your lamp trimmed and full of oil so that you are ready for his return.

No one knows the hour at which this will happen. So be alert at all times and avoid anything of which you would be ashamed in my presence. I will come again and gather you to myself, beloved, because you belong to my Kingdom.

Col. 1:13; Col. 2:15; Matt. 25:1–13; 1 Thess. 5:1–11.

134

Be Always Ready

—— o ——

"Be dressed ready for service and keep your lamps burning."

(Luke 12:35)

Be careful that no one deceives you. Remember that one of the enemy's characteristics is deception. He will try to deceive even those I have chosen for myself.

To believers some areas of deception are easy to detect. People claim to be false Christs or Messiahs. There are those who always say the end is about to happen because of wars and catastrophes. Jesus warned that such things are bound to happen, but are only birth pains.

There will be times of fear, opposition and persecution as there have been throughout the history of the Church. These test the spiritual temperature of people's hearts. The cold and lukewarm soon fall away, but **those whose hearts are full of love for me and are on fire with my Spirit will stand firm. I** promise that all who stand firm to the end will be saved.

There is coming a time of conflict, turmoil and great distress. For the sake of my beloved ones those days will be shortened. Don't listen to those who claim to have a special revelation about when Jesus will come again. Only I determine that, just as I determined when he came in the flesh.

He will come as suddenly as he left his disciples. There will be many physical phenomena within creation which will accompany his return, not precede it.

When he comes again his glory will be revealed. Don't speculate endlessly about the timing and the means of these events. **Live as one who is prepared so that whenever he returns you will be ready.** Don't be like the foolish servants who were not obeying the master when he returned. Those who are found ready when he returns will be put in charge of all my possessions!

At that time all the nations will be gathered before him and he will separate the people as the shepherd separates the sheep from the goats. Rejoice, my beloved, that you are numbered among those who hear his voice and follow him. Don't live in speculation. Be ready and on the watch. **Jesus will come back for you.**

Matt. 24:4–25; Matt. 24:29–51; 1 Thess. 5:1–11; Rev. 7:13–17.

135

My Glory

———— o ————

"Arise, shine, for your light has come, and the glory of the Lord rises upon you."

(Isa. 60:1)

Peter, James and John were given a very special privilege when they witnessed Jesus' transfiguration. No matter what happened in the coming months, everything would end in glory!

They had to climb the mountain with Jesus. Many are not prepared to climb spiritual heights with me; they want everything to come easily. They expect me to drop continual blessings into their laps regardless of whether they wait on me, believe my word or remain obedient to my purposes.

Sometimes I ask you to climb mountains with me in prayer, setting times aside to wait on me. On other occasions I ask you to give time to attend conferences when I can lead you to spiritual heights where you have not been before. Climbing these mountains involves sacrifice, but leads to great benefits.

On this occasion Jesus' body was transformed in appearance. His face shone like the sun and his clothes became white. As the Messiah, he was the fulfilment of the law and the prophets – represented by Moses and Elijah who appeared with him.

A bright cloud enveloped the disciples and they heard my voice proclaiming that this was my Son in whom I delighted. You can understand Peter wanting to remain bathed in such glory.

That experience was a great encouragement, and yet the disciples failed to grasp the implications of what was happening. Beyond the suffering was the assurance that Jesus would return to the glory from which he came. His life would not end in the cold death of the tomb. He would be raised and restored to the glory that was rightfully his.

Don't be afraid to climb mountains with me, beloved. You, too, will receive revelation of my glory. It is good for you to meet with me during the daily circumstances of your life; but there will be times when I will reveal myself to you in particular ways, which will have a profound effect on you. **I want you to know me in my majesty and glory.** For my children are to speak to this generation about the glory of my Kingdom and tell of my righteousness. And you cannot speak of what you do not know!

Beloved, life cannot be a continuous mountain-top experience; but you need revelation to sustain and encourage you, especially through trying and testing times.

Matt. 17:1–6; Isa. 40:29–31; Ps. 18:33; Ps. 145:10–13.

136

Treasure in Heaven

———— ○ ————

"For where your treasure is, there your heart will be also."

(Luke 12:34)

Where does your treasure lie, child? In the bank? In your possessions? Do you find your security in what you have, or in me?

Whatever belongs to this life is corruptible. If the purpose of your life is to acquire worldly possessions you are to be pitied, for you have not understood the priorities of my Kingdom.

Store up treasure in heaven where nothing is corruptible. There the enemy cannot steal from you.

Beloved, your salvation is assured for you have put your faith in what Jesus did for you on the cross. But I want you to have the best possible reward as well as the salvation of your soul. And I have made it clear that I reward each person for what he or she has done. This is why I want the work of my Kingdom to be the priority in your life.

You have resources you can channel into the work of my Kingdom. **Give where your money will truly be used effectively for my Kingdom.** If your heart is in the work of my Kingdom, that is where you will invest your treasure.

A wise man doesn't sow good seed in a desert; the seed would only go to waste. It would produce nothing despite its quality. The money you give is seed. Sow it in good soil where it will be productive and fruitful. Then my Kingdom will benefit and you will receive the blessing I promise to those who are faithful in their giving.

There will always be those who suggest it is unspiritual to talk about money. If that is true, Jesus would be unspiritual, for he often spoke about money! Those who are afraid of the subject obviously have something to hide!

I want you to support by prayer and giving those working for the extension of my Kingdom. And I want you to use every opportunity to be involved yourself in this work, even if it requires making sacrifices. You will be amply rewarded.

I promise to give back abundantly to those who give to me. Why? Because their giving is an expression of their loving obedience and faith in my word.

Yes, beloved, wherever your treasure is, there will your heart be also.

Matt. 6:19–20; Matt. 16:27; 2 Cor. 8:7; 2 Cor. 9:6.

137

Use My Resources

———— o ————

"Well done, good and faithful servant! You have been faithful with a few things; I will put you in charge of many things. Come and share in your master's happiness!"

(Matt. 25:23)

My dear son, understand what I have entrusted to you. I have not only endowed you with natural gifts but also with spiritual ones. I have given you a rich inheritance, not to waste or squander but to use to the full. You will have to give account to me personally for the way you have used what has been entrusted to you.

In the parable of the talents it is clear that I don't want you selfishly to hide my gifts, nor refrain from using them because you fear making mistakes.

See how I congratulate those who put their gifts to the right use. They have proved themselves faithful. They have shown that I can entrust them with more and more. **They have proved faithful in small things; I can therefore give them responsibility for greater things**

And what is their reward? The faithful ones can share in my joy, a joy that is eternal.

Are you perplexed that the lazy servant knew me to be one who harvests where he has not sown and gathers where he has not scattered seed? Does this seem unjust to you, beloved?

I send my children to sow and scatter the seed of my word. I have given them my word that they may take it to every part of the world. I expect them to do this. Every believer is to share the word of truth with others. I don't want any to hide his light under the table.

The sharing of that word with others gives you a greater confidence in that word yourself. You have found this in your own experience, haven't you, child? **Every time you speak my truth to others you are even more convinced of the truth yourself.** And your understanding of my word is enlarged at the same time.

It is good to study my word. But there is little point in a farmer studying his seed if he doesn't sow it! Having discovered that the seed is good he sows it in anticipation of a good harvest. However, he knows he will not reap an instantaneous harvest. He will have to wait for the growth process to take place before the crop is ready for harvest.

Look around you; there is a rich harvest waiting to be reaped. This is because others have sown the seed of my word and you can now reap the benefit of their labours.

In the same way others will reap the harvest of what you sow. Don't be proud, therefore, when you reap. Others have often shared in the labour. And don't be discouraged when you sow and see little immediate fruit. Believe that what is sown will come to harvest, even if others do the reaping!

And remember, child, one sows, another reaps, but it is I who cause the seed to grow. The whole process would be ineffective without me.

It would not happen without you either; don't you see this? I treated the lazy servant harshly because I can't give growth to what has not been sown. The seed is ineffective until it is put into the ground. We have to work together, don't we, child?

The lazy servant had the seed taken from him and given to the one who would put it to good use!

Matt. 25:14–30; 1 Cor. 1:7; Luke 8:16; John 4:35; Philem. 6.

138

The Great Commission

———— o ————

"All authority in heaven and on earth has been given to me. Therefore go and make disciples of all nations, baptising them in the name of the Father and of the Son and of the Holy Spirit, and teaching them to obey everything I have commanded you."

(Matt. 28:18–20)

Before Jesus returned to my glory in heaven, he gave the emerging Church a great commission. He made it clear that he had all authority in heaven and on earth. So the command he gave to the disciples had this immense authority behind it.

What did he tell his Church to do? They were to do three things: **First, they were to make disciples of all nations.** They were not to look only for an initial response to the gospel. They were to build the converts in faith and love, to oversee the growth of the seed of my Kingdom sown in their hearts when they turned to me in repentance and faith.

True disciples believe my word; they walk in my love and reach out to others in my name. Despite their imperfections they are my witnesses demonstrating how to live the life of my Kingdom here on earth.

Secondly, those first disciples were told to baptise those who responded to the gospel. That act of immersion in water signifies that their old former life was dead and buried. They had died and their lives were now hidden with Christ in me! They were free to live the new life.

Thirdly, having led them through baptism, they were to teach them to obey everything Jesus commanded those first disciples. Yes, beloved, *everything.*

Every command given to those first disciples is a command to my disciples today. They are to preach that my Kingdom is at hand. I have given them authority to drive out evil spirits and to heal every disease and sickness. They can even raise the dead.

And Jesus promised to be with his disciples until the end of the age to enable them to do these things. **I expect, therefore, all these things of my Church today. My commission to my Church has not changed.**

You have received freely from me, beloved. As a disciple of Jesus go and share the life of the gospel with others. Be assured, I am with you. Scatter the seed of my word. Encourage disciples with the truth and know that you have my power and authority to overcome all the power of the evil one.

Rom. 6:3–4; Mark 16:15–18; Matt. 28:20.

139

Will You Speak For Me?

———— ○ ————

"'My house will be called a house of prayer for all nations.' But you have made it a 'den of robbers'."

(Mark 11:17)

S ometimes I use my authority in judgment. Jesus cleared the temple of those who defiled it with their trade, deception and fraud. This surprised those who saw it and aroused attitudes of resentment in the religious leaders.

Beloved, my temple needs cleansing today. Whenever people speak openly against things that dishonour me in the life of my Church, they will be met with similar reactions to those Jesus experienced from ecclesiastical authorities! They will arouse bitter opposition and deep resentment. They will be accused of setting themselves up as judges when they are faithfully declaring my word!

My word judges the actions of all my people. It is sharper than a double-edged sword, cutting to the division of soul and spirit.

I want to revive my Church because I love the Body of my Son. I don't want to judge but to bless. My word will show what is of the Spirit, that which I have initiated, and what is soulish, coming from man.

Some leaders are concerned more for their own welfare than for my precious ones. They are like the hirelings Jesus spoke of, who flee at the first signs of trouble. They leave the wolf to do its work. It is time to cleanse his Body of such leadership. I want leaders who will defend the flock against the ravishes of the enemy, no matter whether his attacks come from without or within. I want leaders who will lead my children to rich pastures and enable them to fulfil the ministries to which I call them.

I want to cleanse my Church of unbelief; to see a return to faith in my word. **I want to cleanse it of worldly practices,** money raising and immorality. And yet I love my Church despite its spots and wrinkles, because my Church is people; and I love people.

Because his Body consists of individuals, the cleansing has to be done in each member. The whole cannot be cleansed unless each individual is cleansed. I don't want professionals; I want disciples. I don't want religious people, but followers of the Way. I don't want tea parties; I want evangelism. I don't want money-raising; I want faithful giving!

Who will speak for me? Who will speak out against things that defile the temple? Will you, beloved?

Mark 11:15–18; Heb. 4:12; John 10:11–13.

140

Name Above All Names

——— o ———

"Therefore God exalted him to the highest place and gave him the name that is above every name."

(Phil. 2:9)

The name of Jesus is all-powerful. You have authority to use his name.

One day, Peter and John healed the cripple who begged at the temple gate. They didn't have money to give the beggar. But they did have the authority to heal in Jesus' name. So they commanded him to rise and walk in the name of Jesus. He sprang to his feet, began to walk and jump, praising me as he did so.

As you can imagine this created quite a stir and once again it was the religious ones who didn't like what had happened. The apostles made it clear to all: **"By faith in the name of Jesus, this man whom you see and know was made strong. It is Jesus' name and the faith that comes through him that has given this complete healing to him, as you can all see."**

Jesus is the same yesterday, today and for ever and he was continuing his ministry through those apostles. And that same ministry continues in his Church today. Has the name of Jesus lost any of its power? Is not his name still the name that is above every other name?

Many in positions of great distress have called on the name of Jesus to save them in moments of crisis and danger. They have immediate deliverance as a result. Others know they can live in the protection of that name; when they do, they are shielded by my power.

Use the name of Jesus. Those who belong to the world blaspheme his name; **those who belong to my Kingdom use his name to triumph,** by faith they know they have overcome the world. Every day of their lives they call upon the name of Jesus.

Remember, beloved, that I have exalted above all things my name and my word.

Whatever you do, in word or deed, do it all in the name of the Lord Jesus Christ, giving thanks to me through him. When you speak or act in his name, you do these things on my behalf. It is as if he is doing them in and through you. Isn't it wonderful that I give you such privilege, beloved?

You can do what he would do, say what he would say, pray what he would pray, believe what he would believe. And when you do so, you will receive similar results!

Acts 3:1–10,16; Heb. 13:8; Ps. 138:2; Col. 3:17.

141

Bring Me Glory

———— ○ ————

"This is to my Father's glory, that you bear much fruit, showing yourselves to be my disciples."

(John 15:8)

Jesus was questioned concerning a man who was born blind, whether his infirmity was a result of his sin or that of his parents. He replied that neither was the cause of the blindness. The man's healing was going to bring me glory.

My nature is not revealed in sickness or sin; neither glorifies me. I am glorified in every act of forgiveness, healing and deliverance. Jesus came to reveal my glory and to save men from their sickness, sin and bondage. Every time he did such things I was glorified.

I am glorified whenever you rejoice in me in the face of adversity. I am glorified as I see you walking by faith, speaking to mountains of need, commanding them to be moved. I am glorified when you resist the attacks of Satan and he flees from you, when you refuse to accept the negative accusations others bring against you.

And I am glorified in every life you touch with my power and love. The more fruit you bear through the power of my Holy Spirit working in your life in practical, tangible ways, the more I am glorified in you.

Some people put limitations on me which did not exist in Jesus' ministry. When people came to him for healing, he wanted only to know if they had faith that he would be glorified in the healing of the sickness. He knew what my will was in relation to healing and he was concerned for my glory in every situation.

Beloved, whenever you pray or minister in my name, let my glory be your motive, that I might be glorified both in you and in those you serve.

John 9:1–3; John 15:7–8; John 14:12–14.

142

My Family

——— ○ ———

"Both the one who makes men holy and those who are made holy are of the same family. So Jesus is not ashamed to call them brothers."

(Heb. 2:11)

Ever since you were born again you have been part of my family. I adopted you as my very own child when you put your faith in Jesus.

His mother and brothers searched for him while he was teaching. When told of their arrival, he made it clear he had a different concept of family. His relatives were those who did his will! And his will is to believe in him!

You, child, have me as your Father and Jesus as your brother! All who are born again are your brothers and sisters, irrespective of race or denomination. This is an entirely different view of family from the usual worldly understanding.

Jesus taught that anyone who loves his father or mother, wife and children, brothers and sisters more than him is not worthy of him and cannot be his disciple. Anyone who fails to take up his cross and follow him is not worthy of him. Does this seem harsh? Well, he was making it clear that his will must come first at all times.

Of course he wants you to love your family, but not to idolise them or allow your love for them to stand in the way of your obedience to him. There can be conflict sometimes, can't there?

Those who are wise know that if they place me first they will bring blessing to their families. I won't cause them to neglect their families, neither will I let their loved ones suffer through their obedience to me.

I don't view my Church as an organisation or structure, but as a family of believers, a holy people who delight to do my will; a people who submit to my Lordship at all times.

You are part of that family, child. Fulfil your responsibilities to your natural family; but understand you also have wider responsibilities to the household of faith to which you belong. You can be sure that I shall cause my righteous ones to flourish and be exceedingly fruitful!

Eph. 1:5; Matt. 12:46–50; Matt. 10:37–8; Ps. 128:1–4; Gal. 6:10.

143

Be United

———— ○ ————

"Make my joy complete by being like-minded, having the same love, being one in spirit and purpose."
(Phil. 2:2)

I hate division among my children, caused by criticism and judgment of one another. There should be no jealousy or rivalry among them, but an acknowledgment of each other's distinctive gifts.

Pray for unity among all those born of my Spirit. I live in each of them, and they live in me. That is the basis of unity. All who are one in me are your brothers and sisters. **You possess the same life; you have the same Holy Spirit, you are part of the same Kingdom.** Even though you may not agree on every point of doctrine, you have the same love, my love, with which to encourage and honour one another.

It is easy to see areas of refining needed in others' lives. Their culture may be different from yours; they may express their love for me in different forms of worship from those you enjoy. Nevertheless you have unity in me, a unity which only my Spirit can produce.

Unity cannot be created by outward conformity to religious practices; it cannot be achieved around a conference table. It is the work of my Spirit.

The world will know that I sent Jesus to be its Saviour when it sees Christians affirming one another, rather than destroying each other. This is why he prayed for unity among all those who believe in him. People will be encouraged to believe that there is no other name by which a man can be saved when they see unity among those who profess my name.

I never ask you to compromise the truth. Some separate themselves from others because they believe they have a better grasp of the truth. Jesus didn't do that. He mingled with those who needed the truth!

Beloved, his body will continue to experience the suffering Jesus experienced. There will still be rejection from those who refuse to believe in me, opposition from those who worship false gods. **Don't be discouraged. The truth will be victorious.** So hold fast to the truth, share it with others and rejoice in the way you see them being set free!

1 Cor. 12:12–27; John 17.20–3; John 13:34–5.

144

Jesus Is The Only Way

———— o ————

**"I am the way and the truth and the life. No-one comes
to the Father except through me."**

(John 14:6)

B eloved, you live in a world where there is increasing
conflict between my way and other philosophies
and religions. Christians were first called "followers of
The Way". You are a follower of the only way to God.

Stand fearlessly against those who try to compromise
that position. I will not stand for people acknowledging
any other god. I am the only true God. Men cannot
worship me and demons. They cannot follow the truth
and deception at the same time. It is not loving to
compromise with other religions which cause people to
be deceived.

Deception is a form of bondage. Reach out with the
truth to those who are deceived, so they can be liberated
from their bondage. Many who follow a false way
imagine they will have salvation. Yet they don't have
my life now, neither do they have my promise of eternal
life.

When you proclaim the truth you will be accused
of bigotry and intolerance. Jesus suffered such insults
because he claimed to be the only Way and the Truth.
If men hated him, they will hate you also. **You don't**

love those who are deceived by agreeing with them, but by offering the life I can give them.

Jesus said clearly that everyone who listens to me and learns from me comes to him. Listen, child, if anyone loves me, he or she will love my Son also!

You are one of my saints. I warn you that those who follow other gods will war against the saints.

Jesus was dogmatic in his teaching, and intolerant of those who tried to undermine the truth he proclaimed. Yet he still held out the hands of love to any who turned to him. To all who receive him, to those who believe in his name, he gives the right to become children of God.

Declare the truth in love. You will find that many who oppose the truth are themselves intolerant and dogmatic, lacking the love that can be expressed only through my Spirit. Some will realise the truth of what you are saying, and will turn to me.

The question is this, beloved child. **Do you love others sufficiently to confront them with the truth,** no matter what their opinions or religious ideas?

Acts 4:12; 1 John 4:1–6; John 1:12–13.

145

My Peace

———— o ————

"Peace I leave with you; my peace I give you."
(John 14:27)

B eloved, I am your peace. Jesus came as the Prince of
Peace and peace was his parting gift to his disciples.

On the night of his arrest, the disciples needed his
promise of peace. After the crucifixion when they were
shut away in fear, Jesus appeared to them in his risen
body. He stood among them and said: "Peace be with
you." This was not simply a greeting but an imparting
of peace to them.

The world offers temporary peace, simply a respite
from conflict and turmoil. Those who have experienced
new birth know my peace; forgiveness of their sins
restores them to a relationship of peace with me.

I am your peace, beloved. Sin causes you to lose your
sense of peace with me, doesn't it? However, the assurance of my forgiveness silences the inner voice of accusation and condemnation, and your peace is restored.
The guilt is washed away so completely it is as if the sin
had never been committed.

**Peace I leave with YOU. My peace I give to YOU.
Not as the world gives, but my peace.** Don't let anything destroy that peace. Stand against everything in

your life that causes you to lose your peace with me. You will soon discover what those things are. Have nothing to do with them.

When you obey my word you have peace because you are at one with my purposes. If you step outside my purposes you lose that sense of peace. Then you have to begin to justify the decisions you make or the things you do. Beloved, **real peace is to know that all is well between your God and yourself!**

You share in my commission to spread the gospel of peace. You are conscious of many who need to know my peace, their lives torn apart by internal conflict and guilt. **How beautiful are the feet of those who spread the gospel of peace!**

John 14:27; Phil. 4:6–7; 2 Thess 3:16; Isa. 52:7.

146

You Are Mine

———— o ————

"Having believed, you were marked in him with a seal, the promised Holy Spirit, who is a deposit guaranteeing our inheritance until the redemption of those who are God's possession."

(Eph. 1:13–14)

Whether you are an apostle, prophet, evangelist, pastor, teacher, healer, worker of miracles, administrator or helper, you are in my Son and he is in you. And you have the responsibility of living his life as a witness in the world.

Be ready to go wherever I lead you and do whatever I ask of you. You will never regret your obedience to me. Many others will give glory and thanks to me because of the impact of your life on them.

Beloved, there are no passengers in the company I lead in triumphal procession.

You are blessed because your eyes see and your ears hear. I have opened your eyes to the truth. Because you are my child, you can hear my voice and be led by my Spirit. Be thankful, therefore, for the glory belongs to me.

Many prophets and righteous men have longed to see what you see but did not see it, and to hear what you hear but did not hear it.

Jesus is the coming King. He will come in majesty and glory, in the splendour of holiness with angels in his train. He will gather those who belong to him.

You are numbered among the elect, child. I have chosen you. My hand is on your life. You live in me and I in you. I hold the destiny of nations in my hands, but never lose sight of any individual, including you!

I am the Alpha and the Omega – the beginning and ending of all things. I spoke and creation came into being. **And everything will find its fulfilment in me.** There will come the time when all that does not belong to me shall pass away.

Isn't it good to know that you are safe and secure in me? **I have made you mine, dear precious child!**

Luke 10:23–4; Mark 13:26–7; 1 Pet. 1:1–2; Rev. 1:8.